Edna,
Best Wishes
Stay young!
[signature]

02/26/2012

Fighting the Effects of Gravity

A Bittersweet Journey into Middle Life

James Robinson Jr.

iUniverse, Inc.
Bloomington

Fighting the Effects of Gravity
A Bittersweet Journey into Middle Life

Copyright © 2012 by James Robinson Jr.

All rights reserved. No part of this book may be used or reproduced by any means, graphic, electronic, or mechanical, including photocopying, recording, taping or by any information storage retrieval system without the written permission of the publisher except in the case of brief quotations embodied in critical articles and reviews.

The views expressed in this work are solely those of the author and do not necessarily reflect the views of the publisher, and the publisher hereby disclaims any responsibility for them.

iUniverse books may be ordered through booksellers or by contacting:

iUniverse
1663 Liberty Drive
Bloomington, IN 47403
www.iuniverse.com
1-800-Authors (1-800-288-4677)

Because of the dynamic nature of the Internet, any web addresses or links contained in this book may have changed since publication and may no longer be valid. The views expressed in this work are solely those of the author and do not necessarily reflect the views of the publisher, and the publisher hereby disclaims any responsibility for them.

Any people depicted in stock imagery provided by Thinkstock are models, and such images are being used for illustrative purposes only. Certain stock imagery © Thinkstock.

ISBN: 978-1-4620-6984-2 (sc)
ISBN: 978-1-4620-6986-6 (hc)
ISBN: 978-1-4620-6985-9 (e)

Printed in the United States of America

iUniverse rev. date: 1/12/2012

This book is, in no small part, a result of the unending love and support of my immediate family and my faith in God. I also wish to offer special thanks to Dr. Isabel Beck. I couldn't have done it without you.

Contents

In a Nutshell ix

Chapter 1: A Word to the Wise. 1

SECTION ONE
When a Good Body Goes Bad 7

Chapter 2: The Day My Butt Said Good-Bye 9
    Don't Cry for Me, Mr. Gravity 18

Chapter 3: Oh, My Aching Body. 31

Chapter 4: Middle-Age Sex. 41

Chapter 5: The Agony of the Feet 49

Chapter 6: They Call It Presbyopia, but It's Still a
Pair of Bifocals to Me 55

Chapter 7: What's Up, Doc? 61

SECTION TWO
Getting into the Middle-Aged Head 69

Chapter 8: I Can See a Little Too Clearly Now 71

Chapter 9: Wake Me When It's Over. 77

Chapter 10: Or Is It Chapter 9? I Forget. 87
    Putting a Face on the Brain Cramp. 87

Chapter 11: Beware the Middle-Age Dance. 95

Chapter 12: I Don't Want to Get Old, and You
Can't Make Me! 103
    I Can't Bear to Watch .113
    Go Forth in Peace 118

Chapter 13: What Do You Mean I Have to Die? 121
    How Will It Happen? .130
    Where to Put It? 135
    The Wake-Up Call. 141

Chapter 14: They Don't Call It Baggage for Nothin' 149
    Oh, All Right Then. But Do We Really Have to
    Call It Baggage? 156

Chapter 15: Life Sucks and Then They Give You a
Wristwatch. 161
    So Much for That Meaning of Life Notion 168
    The Liberation. And a Big Shout-Out to Jimmy Durante172

In a Nutshell

My full name is James J. Robinson Jr., and I'd like to introduce you to my labor of love—*Fighting the Effects of Gravity: A Bittersweet Journey into Middle Life*. *Fighting the Effects of Gravity* is a humorous account of my fifty-eight years of living and, in particular, my foray into the world of midlife.

I'm what you might call a late bloomer. Consider the fact that I'm practically a senior citizen and I'm just getting around to finishing my first book. I attended Carnegie Mellon University and graduated in 1974 with a degree in English and aspirations of becoming the next Kurt Vonnegut. I went on to get married in 1976 and father three children, all girls, in the span of four years—oops, so much for that dream.

My children didn't allow their father much time to become an author; far from it—they wouldn't allow their father much time to sleep. As their numbers mounted, a pattern emerged. One by one they joined the "let's keep Daddy from writing" fraternity. They cried all night—begging for food or diaper changes—and then slept like angels when family and friends huddled around, admired them, and tried to guess which one of us they looked like the most. In their prime, all three little ladies were in diapers at the same time, going through almost two hundred cloth diapers per week.

Forced to put my writing career on hold to feed my family, I could never really get an alternate career going. One look at my résumé will tell you that I never quite found my niche. Even a degree from a prestigious university like CMU isn't marketable when William Shakespeare and Eugene O'Neill are your wingmen.

I count seven jobs in my forty-six-year vocational journey. There were others, but they were so short-lived that I strategically buried them in the archives of my work history, left with no consistency in my experience and no one job on which I could build a foundation. In fact, if you put all of my varied positions in a room, they would not really have much to say to one another.

But it was the position I held as a benefits analyst at the University of Pittsburgh in 1988 that is most important to this story—not so much because of the duties performed but because of the physical transformations that occurred during this time. For it was during the years I spent at Pitt signing up staff and faculty for university benefits that I first began to feel the effects of what I came to know as middle age.

In 1994, with the kids growing up and my sleep deprivation on the decline, I began to pursue my passion, documenting my midlife experiences in earnest. The funny thing is that I couldn't write about midlife until I reached midlife, a bit of a Catch-22, I guess. The results of my experiences are documented here.

My book, *Fighting the Effects of Gravity: A Bittersweet Journey into Middle Life*, is a graphic, unabashed account of my head-on collision with the immovable object known as middle age. Using my own middle-age adventures as a point of reference, I will give you an uncensored look at the creature known as midlife from the inside out, hopefully providing for you that much-needed handbook and Swiss Army knife that no one ever bothered to bestow upon me.

I will offer no cute little games, no clever primers, no questionnaires, no silly tests that claim to qualify you for midlife membership—just some useful tips from the point of view of someone who suddenly finds himself in a war of wills with the aging process. In short, a mature but anxious fifty-eight-year-old man who often wonders aloud if God has forsaken him and why he has apparently auctioned his aging soul to the highest bidder. I'll present my story in two parts, because in my opinion, the tangible signs of middle age can best be broken into two very distinct categories: mental and physical. I will begin with the physical embodiments, because unlike their more subtle mental counterparts, they tend to grab all of the attention, usually involving dramatic, tangible signs of decay.

You'll be introduced to such topics as old age, death, and mental deterioration in a humorous and sometimes poignant manner. Don't be frightened. It is not my intent to put the fear of God in you but rather to give you a little something for the road, some much-needed food for thought. My goal is not to ruin your weekend but to keep you smiling long enough to get you over the hump. After all, there's nothing particularly ominous or sinister about middle age. It's merely the next stage, part two in the three-part story of life.

I see midlife as a wake-up call, a Post-it note from God telling you to get your life in order. Middle life won't be the death of you. Something much more noteworthy will come along to take care of that, so I see no reason why we can't laugh at it together. As my mother often says when we treat some small setback as if it were an earth-shattering event, "There's nothing eternal about it." So, as you read on, grab your roses or your coffee or whatever you want to smell and keep in mind that there's nothing eternal about this thing known as midlife.

As the maître d' says in one of my favorite *Three Stooges* episodes: "Follow me, and walk this way ..."

Chapter 1: A Word to the Wise

Despite any physical or mental problems that I may outline on the following pages, know that we middle-agers have the final laugh in this little game. In the scheme of things, the physical setbacks that signal the end of our youth aren't really worth trashing hours of precious sleep.

In the big picture, our physical ailments should be considered nothing more than an annoyance or a minor setback. There are just too many other more serious physical pitfalls out there for us to get too excited about a few aches and pains. Not that I'm minimizing our plight; the physical problems that beset individuals in midlife are a very real concern. But we have to be realistic. In the big picture, we don't have a lot to complain about.

What's more important is that we don't have to grin and bear it alone. We have a network of fellow baby boomers with whom we can share our grief. Whether we know it or not, those of us marooned in this middle section of life, we forty- and fifty-somethings, males and females, share a unique camaraderie, a special bond.

Being a member of this embattled group of individuals reminds me of my younger days, when I was a single, carefree twenty-two-year-old and had the opportunity to purchase my dream car, a 1975 Corvette convertible.

As a new owner, I couldn't understand why other Corvette owners, as they approached me driving in the opposite direction, would signal by honking their horns, waving, or flashing their headlights. Eventually I realized that these acts were gestures of goodwill, like a secret handshake, their way of acknowledging another "Vette" owner. Such is the esprit de corps that surrounds this celebrated vehicle. In fact, simply saying the word "Corvette" could elicit o-o-hs and a-a-a-hs from an adoring public. I had bought into a secret society without realizing it. I eventually had to part with the car—my dream turned out to be a mechanical nightmare—but my infatuation with the sleek Chevy continues.

I see the same type of unspoken comradeship among the ranks of the middle-aged. We can pass another member of this distinguished club on the street and, without even the symbolic wave or honking horn, still have a sense of what the other is going through.

I remember moving my middle child, Erin, into her college dorm—she is now an RN. If you have ever been involved with college moving day in a large university, I'm sure you understand my plight: parents and soon-to-be-students all vying for the same thing—to get their children's belongings into their rooms as quickly as possible and without incurring any serious injuries.

The line for the elevators was so long and these overburdened conveyors so slow on this day that many of us had no choice but to use the stairs to transport items. I even had enough foresight to bring along a dolly to cart the heavier items. Erin's room, as Murphy's Law might suggest, was on the fifth floor. So much for planning ahead.

I must have made ten or more trips up and down those five flights of stairs, toting everything from clothing and stuffed animals to a large plastic storage bin full of shoes and a small refrigerator and microwave oven. My lovely daughter also felt the need to bring along over twenty pairs of jeans. You'll note that this type of information never finds its way into anyone's wedding vows: "Do you promise to love, honor, obey, and carry all of your college-bound child's belongings up five flights of stairs or until

Fighting the Effects of Gravity

exhaustion renders you unable to stand or speak?" Some things are better left unsaid.

I consider myself to be in pretty good shape, but I certainly wasn't prepared for this contest of endurance. I had to wonder how those in lesser shape prevailed, how the chain-smoking, couch-potato parents were handling the strain. I almost felt as if I were being tested by the university to see if I could handle the rigors of college life from a parent's perspective before they admitted me.

Given this scenario, perhaps the college could have devised a whole schedule of athletic events for us parents to compete in—a middle-aged parent's version of that one-on-one competitive show *American Gladiators*, perhaps. How about a joust between two paunchy middle-agers standing on a supine unstable log, poking at one another with long poles? The loser falls into a pool of water below. Why not make us scale a ten-foot-high wall with a rope, or run through one of those tire-agility drills?

How about volunteers stationed along the route, cheering us on, exhorting us to get all of the belongings moved, handing us cups of water like bystanders at marathon races: "Come on, you with the microwave! Let's go! Just one more flight!" Or "You, carrying the twenty pairs of jeans, suck it up, you can do it!"

Pardon my sarcasm, but it was during this marathon event that I realized what middle-aged parents go through with college-aged children. Coming up with the tuition is obviously just the beginning.

As we midlifers passed one another—sweating like marathon runners and carrying ironing boards, new computers, and area rugs and gasping for breath on the stairs—we never had to say a word. We were probably too exhausted to speak anyway. We simply nodded or managed a painful smile to each other as we passed time and time again on the stairs, as if to say, "I'm going to have a heart attack. I can't believe I'm going through all this to get my kid into college."

In this way, each of us can silently salute the other's accomplishments. We can applaud one another, secure in the knowledge that we have survived to reach the halfway point. Each of us can pat the other on the back in celebration of the fact that we have paid our dues.

Our bodies may be on the decline, but we have one huge advantage over our youthful counterparts. We are the survivors, the veterans of this battle. We have the wisdom of forty or more years on our sides. Our résumés are brimming with life experience. We see life from a far more mature vantage point than the average youngster does.

Besides, who among you would really want to be twenty-one again? Granted, life probably treated you with more respect when you were younger. Sure, Mother Nature seems to smile on the young and treat us noble half-centurions with disdain. Of course, our body parts are moving closer to the equator with each passing minute, and we have to work twice as hard to lose a pound as we did in our youth.

However, we can look at the average twenty-one-year-old and realize that, despite their firm stomachs, upright breasts, and seemingly never-ending supply of hormones, they don't have a clue as to what life is about. They take their blessings for granted. These youngsters won't truly appreciate the advantages that youth affords them until it begins to slip away. As Joni Mitchell sang, "You don't know what you've got til it's gone."

And I know that, whatever maturity they might possess, they are still looking up from the bottom rung of life's ladder. Our children, as fast as they seem to grow up these days, are still children, still struggling to find their way. There are so many lessons yet to learn, lessons that can only be taught by life's system of hard knocks.

We midlifers, on the other hand, are in our prime, enjoying our best years in many ways. I like to think that the majority of us have matured with age. We're seasoned like a fine wine when it comes to distinguishing between what is and what isn't important in life. We have learned, by this stage of the game, not to waste our time "sweating the small stuff" but rather to save our energy for the bigger tests that will come our way somewhere along the line.

I seem to have developed this mature voice of reason that calms me down in stressful situations and helps me to keep things in perspective. "Don't get excited," the voice says. "This is not a big deal. Being told you have cancer could be considered a big deal. But you can deal with such shocking news also. This will all be over soon." Of course, sometimes this voice is just a little too rational for its own good and gets on my nerves. There are times when I am forced to tell the voice to shut up, that I'll get all bent out of shape if that's what I want to do.

It is in our forties and fifties when we finally realize how important it is to laugh and how necessary it is to cry. We know that our battles with the ravages of middle age will only make us more resolved, more determined in the long run. We have come to believe in the popular axiom "What doesn't kill you only makes you stronger."

My wife and I get together with middle-aged friends and have truly meaningful conversations. It doesn't even seem to matter if the friends are in their fifties or sixties; life experiences prevail. We vacation with my parents and enjoy their company, and they are in their early eighties.

We're all pretty much bailing water from the same leaky boat, having walked the same tightrope in the same shoes. If the friends happen to be older, their wisdom can act as a sneak peek into the very-near future. We compare notes about our parents and our in-laws and our kids. They can relate to us and give us advice on how to deal with certain situations, and we can do the same for them because we all know the score. We no longer have to theorize about what life is about like we did in our youth.

Above all, we can share a determination never to shrink from a confrontation with our nemesis, the master of disaster, the Sultan of Swat known as midlife. After the failure of an integral body part, we will always come out swinging. We can sneer in the face of our antagonist and let him know we can take anything he can dish out. Our once proud "stuff" may be slipping, but our spirits are on the rise. "Come on, Mr. Gravity," we can taunt in our fiercest voice, "is that all you've got?"

SECTION ONE

When a Good Body Goes Bad

Chapter 2: The Day My Butt Said Good-Bye

HAVE YOU EVER NOTICED that there are these weird souls walking the earth, twisted beings who have a habit of using the word "mister" in front of every noun, especially when they speak to their children? If, in fact, these individuals do exist, it would do my heart good to actually see one in the flesh. Such is the profound impact that they have had on my life. Not a day goes by, it seems, that I don't ponder their actuality.

Surely at some point in your existence you have heard strange statements such as these emanating from the mouths of adults: "Come on, Johnny, we're going bye-byes. Let's put on *Mr. Jacket*." "We don't want to trip and fall! Shouldn't we tie *Mr. Shoe*?" "Eat *Mr. Asparagus*! You want to grow up to be big and strong, don't you?" "Now, Billy, tell Mommy when you have to go tee-tee. Don't pull on *Mr. Penis!*" Chatting with one such individual, at this point, would be tantamount to exchanging barbs with a legend, not unlike sitting down to tea and crumpets with the ever-elusive Bigfoot.

I don't recall my parents ever speaking to me in such a condescending manner, but there must be culprits out there somewhere. I see you trying to hide. I demand that you show yourselves!

Don't laugh! No one is truly innocent here. How many times have you schooled your children on the dangers of the toxic menace by placing one of those emphatic little ugly-face stickers everywhere you stored cleaning supplies? I understand that researchers actually polled a group of children while designing the sticker and asked them which color and which face they found to be the most offensive. What is that lovable but vile little fellow's name? Isn't it ... Mr. Yuk? Okay, not quite the same thing, but close!

Even the corporate world has gotten into the act. Why would anyone—unless they were of a certain suspicious mind-set—name their coffee maker Mr. Coffee or market their cleaning solution under the name Mr. Clean? Why, for the love of God, would a company want to coin their outdoor portable toilet Mr. John? How about the culinary expert who provides cooking tips to millions of TV viewers and goes by the name Mr. Food?

You see, for years now, I have been attaching the Mister prefix to just about any noun that would stand still long enough to be lured into my web. I knew no shame. I would direct full-grown adults to close "Mr. Door." I cautioned my teenage girls to wash "Mr. Hands" before dinner or warned them that there would be no dessert unless they cleaned "Mr. Plate." From the time they were toddlers, I threatened my children with a menacing pincer movement featuring my big toe and second toe and calling it "Mr. Lobster." Since my kids are far too old and sophisticated for my antics these days, I am now breaking in my grandchildren. Unfortunately, since they are boys, they could give a rat's hind-end.

I used the Mister prefix for no reason in particular—just a long-running gag, a ploy to get a rise out of my friends and family, an annoyance designed to rattle as many nerves as humanly possible. And it's worked to perfection; just ask any of them.

I meant nothing by it—just a little something to take the edge off. The whole philosophy speaks to my personality. I am what my wife commonly, albeit crudely, refers to as a real "smart ass."

Fighting the Effects of Gravity

I am endowed with a kind of wry, sarcastic, David-Letterman wit, a cynical sense of humor that often makes people either stare at me in puzzlement or smile and shake their heads in disbelief and say, "You're bad!" My heart swells with pride when I elicit this comment. Mission accomplished.

I'll also say or do anything for a laugh. My wife, Debbie, in fact, refuses to laugh at these antics and often advises others to do the same. "Don't laugh at him," she begs those who would even think of reinforcing my subtle attempts at humor. "It will just make him worse."

How could I have known that middle age, the Mister designation, and gravity would one day form an unholy alliance? Who would have suspected that they would join forces in an evil attempt to pound me into submission? How does that old saying go? "What a tangled web we weave ..."

My thoughts take me back to the days of the early children's shows, those ancient forerunners to today's whiz-bang kiddy fare. My earliest recollections center on *Romper Room* and *Captain Kangaroo*, two of my favorite shows from the (gulp) late fifties.

I'm sure many of you sat mesmerized by one of the late-1950s, pre-technology-boom television sets like I did. You probably recall that one worked these televisions like rubbing two sticks together to get a picture going compared to today's state-of-the-art, digital, fifty-five-inch, plasma, LCD (liquid-crystal display), DLP (digital light processing), 3-D, high-definition wonders. By the way, where would technology be without initials?

These television sets also provided only three channels, no color, no remote, a tiny little speaker that sat in until today's state-of-the-art sound systems could be created, and of course, who could forget the forerunner to today's cable systems, the irrepressible "rabbit ears."

James Robinson Jr.

Ah yes, no TV was complete without rabbit ears, that little gizmo, a fixture atop the TV set that required constant adjustment to enable it to boldly, albeit meekly, go out into the airwaves to seek out a signal. If there were a mantra for the brave new world of harnessing TV reception it would no doubt have been "I know you're out there somewhere."

Sometimes, you may recall, a member of the family actually stood by the TV, manually adjusting, more like fidgeting with, the metal rods—the rabbit's ears, if you will—until the picture, like today's army recruit, was the "best that it could be."

More often than not, it was a losing battle. The picture fluctuated between low-grade and high-grade hard-to-see. Remember how we put little pieces of aluminum foil on the tips of the rod-like extensions? What was that about, anyway?

But our expectations were low back then. These days, the quality of a television picture is measured in futuristic language like pixels and lines of resolution. Back in the fifties, the mark of

Fighting the Effects of Gravity

a good picture was determined by whether or not we could make out the images.

In general, it's hard to fathom the astounding leaps that technology has made since we walked the earth in the fifties and early sixties. It's actually difficult to draw comparisons between then and now; it's just not a fair fight. Talk about a time machine. Take this, H. G. Wells.

Perhaps you'll recall that we used rotary telephones for communicating back then. Forget the notion of a personal computer. Computers were in their infancy. There was no such option even when I attended college in the early seventies. I often paid someone to type my theme papers or, if push came to shove, wrote them out in longhand. It pains me to even say that. Computers were of the mainframe variety and occupied entire rooms. Data was represented by holes crudely punched onto cards and then stacked into a bin and sucked into the vast system.

It almost ticks me off the way I can push a button and save a manuscript on both seven hundred fifty gigabytes of hard-drive disk storage space and a four-gigabyte USB "flash drive" when I was forced to write eight-page college papers with an ink pen. I have an iPod that boasts eight gigabytes of space. Who would have believed it?

In the same vein, I have seven hundred photos stored on the compact flash card in my digital camera with space for thousands more. I would never have dreamed this possible when I was taking thirty-six pictures at a time on rolls of celluloid film and storing unused rolls in the refrigerator.

Starbucks, McDonalds, and other establishments lure the laptop generation into their facilities with the offer of "WiFi" Internet availability—the ability to wirelessly stroll about in cyberspace. The meaning is clear: "Come, eat our food, drink our beverages, partake of our computer access. Stay a while. Take your shoes off. Y'all come back now, y'hear?"

Compare the old vinyl record album and its "snap, crackle, pop" sound qualities with MP3 music magic, which isn't even touched by human hands at any point; it's just harnessed, digitally coded, and compressed and then transferred right into your digital audio player at your command like the force in *Star Wars*—nothing to unwrap, nothing to store, nothing to throw away. Amazing!

I can still remember the first time I heard a compact disc in about 1986. I bought one of the first CD players. It was a surreal experience. As Lionel Ritchie sang "Dancing on the Ceiling," I felt as if the music was coming not only from the ceiling, but from all around me. How apropos.

Then we have that one technological breakthrough that best exemplifies how far we've come as a technosociety—a device that harnesses fifty years of aforementioned technology into one neat little package. Yeah, that's right, the cellular telephone, a palm-size, mini-computer marvel.

You have one. I have one. Nowadays, many of us even forsake our home phones in favor of cell phones. Imagine one gadget that accepts those MP3 format digital tunes I spoke of and allows us to takes digital photos; surf the web; check the weather in Madrid, Spain; watch movies; send and receive e-mails and text messages; and access the Internet, which I just met in the late nineties. As Ethel Merman once barked, "Who could ask for anything more?" Oh, and by the way, you can make calls with it too.

Truth is, despite all the modern-day hoopla, I sometimes get a little nostalgic about the so-called good old days. When we had had those three channels and manipulated those rabbit ears we weren't picky. We watched whatever programming was offered, including movies. We didn't have three hundred channels like we do now, but as my wife's friend would say, "We didn't know for nothin'." I remember watching *Saturday Night at the Movies* together as a family. I wonder how many families do that these days.

I have to ask myself, have we come too far? Are we, in fact, in over our electronic heads? Are we brilliant, or is it that we just don't know when to quit? Do we really need to carry on conversations, text our homeys, answer e-mails, watch movies, groove to Lady Gaga and Prince, and check the weather in Zurich while we stand in line at the grocery store? Do innocent bystanders really have to be held captive to our telephone conversations as we stand in long lines at the bank?

I can't help but think about the time when my wife and I were dating and we sat in the car talking and swooning over one another in the Eat'n Park restaurant parking lot. We put our headlights on—a signal that we wanted service—and the waitress came to the car on roller skates to take our order. Our food was placed on a tray, which sat propped up on the car window. I recall how cozy and private it was. We didn't feel the need to hurry home to watch TV or e-mail or text, and neither one of us had a cell phone that threatened to ring to the tune of some obnoxious rap song.

Sometimes I say to myself wistfully, *Take me back to the telephone hung on the wall, to the days of the princess phone, to the days when life was simple and you had to rise from your seat to change the station. Take me back to the days of three channels and the beloved rabbit ears with the mysterious aluminum foil on the antlers.*

Oh, that's a lie. Who am I trying to impress? I like Blu-ray DVD players and sixty-inch DLP and razor-thin LCD TVs and laptops as much as the next guy. I hate to admit it, but I'm a couch potato—I channel surf with the best of them. I just get sick of seeing someone's face stuck in their Android when I'm trying to talk to them. And I don't want to get rear-ended by some sixteen-year-old girl texting her little friend.

I'm climbing out of that time machine as we speak—tight fit.

Now where was I?

Well, if you watched TV back in those prehistoric times, you no doubt recall that *Romper Room* featured the charming Miss Jane, who introduced us to those lovable bees of right and wrong, "Do Bee" and "Don't Bee." It was, "Do Bee a tooth-brusher"; "Don't Bee a bed-wetter," or something to that effect.

But if memory serves me, Miss Jane often summoned a mysterious figure from off camera to provide song and dance.

Yeah, it's all coming back to me now. I can hear her calling his name. "Mr. Music, please!" See what I mean?

Then there was *Captain Kangaroo*. Let's see, old Captain treated us to the charming Mr. Greenjeans; Bunny Rabbit, who, as I recall, would do anything for a carrot; Grandfather Clock, who slept through the proceedings unless we all screamed at him to wake up—"Wake up, Grandfather Clock!"—and the Dancing Bear—not such a great dancer and, given the hindsight of today's sexually enlightened views, a bear in denial, a sensitive soul who had yet to emerge from the closet. Sorry, I had to say it.

Oh, well, strike one. But wait; there are other examples that lend credence to my claims. Surely you remember Mr. Ed, the horse who talked. Or that cute little character from the vintage episodes of *Saturday Night Live*. Mr. Bill, I believe they called him. I still see him in commercials. Remember his famous line: "Oh, no-o-o-o"?

You may question my sanity for beginning my book with such seemingly trivial issues, but there is a definite method to my madness. I consider the preceding exercise a necessary digression to fully explain my predicament.

Further examples of this juvenile Mister practice abound, but if I had to highlight one in particular, I would call as my witness the venerable "Mr. Stick."

Ah, yes, how the name brings back fond memories. Mr. Stick was the name I bestowed upon a small wooden spatula that I brandished for punitive reasons during my children's "formative" years. Suffice it to say that Mr. Stick was my only line of defense during my early years of parenthood, the only obstacle that stood between me and total child anarchy. Pulling Mr. Stick into the fray was like a cop putting out a call for backup. If my youngsters weren't behaving, they knew that the ubiquitous Mr. Stick was standing by, waiting in the wings to dole out justice.

But don't get the wrong idea. I never tortured the tykes. Mr. Stick was, for the most part, a figurehead, a mere symbol of authority. Before you label me a brute or peg me a hard-core child abuser, may I say in my own defense that this tool was a lightweight deterrent constructed of the flimsiest balsa wood and was certainly not invented to be an instrument of pain.

Surely many of you fellow parents had to rely on such a ploy when you were raising your children. I remember my older cousin packing a wooden spoon in her purse to keep her demonic two-year-old son in line when she was forced to take him out in public. (In this instance, it was only marginally effective. He is now middle-aged himself and still marginally demonic.)

In my case, the mere mention of the implement's name was usually enough to garner my kids' attention: "Do I have to get Mr. Stick?" The laws of child-rearing are explicit in this area (look it up if you don't believe me), stating that in such punitive matters, it's often the mere thought that counts.

At any rate, Mr. Stick was not to live a long, full life, succumbing to attrition, a victim of forced retirement. His reign of terror ended when my quick-thinking children, who were always a step ahead of me, drew a cute likeness on him, attaching a pleasant face to the menacing reputation and thus neutralizing his powers—anti-disciplinary Kryptonite; damn those kids!

But every once in a while I would pull my old friend out of my sock drawer and wave him around for old times' sake. I remember the last time fondly. My three daughters—then ages twenty-one, nineteen, and eighteen—shouted in remembrance of their old nemesis, "Mr. Stick!"

I have often wondered if this custom of attaching a sir name to an inanimate object is demonstrated in other cultures. Is there a father in Germany, for instance, who threatens his kinder with Herr Stick if they misbehave? A dad in France who refers to his wooden spoon as Monsieur Stick? And if I were a citizen of Great Britain, would my disciplinary tool, at some point, be in line for the honorary title of Sir Stick? Now where did that come from?

In future years, many other perfectly innocent words and phrases were reduced to gibberish by my insistence on employing the Mister derivation; too many to recall here. But the point is that I saw no harm in it. I considered it a painless diversion and a clever way to ease life's more mundane moments. How was I to know that this irritating habit would come back to bite me in the butt (no pun intended)? That this creature of my own devise would eventually turn and bite its master?

The following story underscores my dilemma. While you might call it the onset of middle age, I consider it a diary of physical betrayal, a tragic case of unsuspecting middle-aged male vs. the wrath of Mother Nature. I'm relating the painful details in the hope that a great many of you out there will be able to find solace in its message. Don't let my continued use of this cute little Mister euphemism fool you; my pain is real. Pardon the pun, but I can think of no better way to describe my circumstance. Ladies and gentlemen, life may be hell, but Mr. Gravity can be a real pain in the butt!

Don't Cry for Me, Mr. Gravity

Hitting the big three-oh was no problem for me. After all, my life seemed fairly uncomplicated, and my body hadn't yet begun to show those telltale signs of wear and tear. I did have weight problems, but not in the way you might think. I remember that, during my teens and twenties, I actually had a surprisingly difficult time maintaining my weight. Believe it or not, I had to *force* myself to eat ice cream, cake, and other goodies just to keep my weight stable. As soon as I hit thirty, this trend seemed to magically reverse itself, but I never thought much of it. If only I had known that my body had initiated a well-conceived battle plan, laying the groundwork for a future assault.

But with no knowledge of the impending skirmish, I looked on the bright side. I relished the fact that I now had a much easier time maintaining and gaining weight. Adding to my positive outlook on the situation was the knowledge that I felt no real physical or mental manifestations of the aging process.

I was an avid weightlifter and considered myself a fairly well-tuned specimen. My muscle tone and development, if I do say so myself, was excellent. My biceps bulged through the confines of clothing designed for mere mortals (I looked especially manly in short-sleeve shirts). My shoulders were quite broad; "too big for the rest of me" was the way one tailor described them. They were so wide that dress shirts had to be custom made to cover them. One of my favorite magazines was *Muscular Development*, which often showcased young bodybuilders such as Arnold Schwarzenegger or Lou Ferrigno of *Incredible Hulk* fame. I always tried to emulate bodybuilders who had that "hourglass" shape: chest at least nine to twelve inches larger than the waist.

Getting myself lined up for a two- or three-piece suit was a bit of a hassle. I had to buy a suit coat large enough to accommodate my upper body. This often meant that the accompanying suit pants—which came with a waist of forty-three inches or so while mine was only thirty-five (most large men are assumed to be portly)—had to be dismantled and recut by a tailor to fit the bottom half of my torso. If a friend or a relative happened to be on hand when I was struggling to find a suit or a jacket to fit my upper torso, I was always a little annoyed when they casually summed up my clothing dilemma with this one trite comment: "Stop lifting weights."

Shy, unassuming individual that I was, I even developed a bit of a Clark Kent/Superman persona. Bodybuilding transformed me from a low-key Clark Kent type into a boldly aggressive and heroic Superman personality, but without the now iconic telephone booth. It seems that I developed this tendency to show off my physique, which belied my quiet demeanor. I could flex my pectoral (chest) muscles on command and make them jump rhythmically to the beat of any moronic little tune that I chanted for effect.

I wore tank tops and sleeveless shirts even under a heavy coat in the dead of winter, just in case. After all, you never can tell when you might have to remove your coat in public. I always had my own set of exercise equipment, including free weights, at my disposal. Even while on vacation, I found a place to work out.

I also made plenty of trips to health-food stores. I ingested those protein supplements and weight-gain products, which increased my caloric intake by 1,200 or so for the purpose of gaining muscular weight. I took pride in the fact that most casual observers presumed that I was ten years younger than my actual age.

I was, in short, a healthy specimen: young, well built, and attractive. I was proud of my body. I had no reason to believe that I wouldn't feel this way forever. But I would soon find out otherwise.

Your stories may differ, but for me, my induction into the fraternity known as middle age began the year I turned thirty-six. It was 1988. My wife and I had just purchased our first house. My children—living, breathing testimonials to the failures of family planning—were ages five, six, and eight and growing faster than I thought humanly possible. I remember friends and family members at the time saying that we were actually lucky to have had children so close in age because we had "gotten them out of the way," and now they could "grow up together."

I appreciated the positive sentiment, but I never quite understood the logic. We never made a conscious decision to even have children, let alone to get the childbearing years "out of the way." And what does "growing up together" have to do with it? Would bringing the little dears into the world at more lengthy intervals have required their being split up and placed in foster homes?

We were living the American dream. To say that we were delighted to become homeowners would be a monumental understatement. Having relocated ten times in the previous ten years, we were beginning to feel like gypsies. Our family was ecstatic to know that at this point in life that, barring any unforeseen circumstances, we could probably go as many as, maybe, five whole years or more without packing up our belongings and moving them to some other location. As it turns out, we have been able to occupy this dwelling for an astounding twenty years!

Despite our euphoria, all was not well. Our financial picture, for one, was definitely not the rosiest. I was working for a local university, which afforded me the luxury of taking graduate classes for $35 a credit, which was, in the scheme of things, next to nothing. But it paid me a salary that bordered on—let's see, all things considered, adjusting for inflation—next to nothing. My wife, meanwhile, had only recently rejoined the party, returning to full-time employment for the first time in our post-baby-boom era.

To be able to close the deal on our modest first home, I had pretty much mortgaged my soul and begged and borrowed money from every family member I felt comfortable begging and borrowing from and some I didn't. Real or imaginary, I was starting to feel the heat. After all, prying a $50,000, thirty-year mortgage from a bank is one thing—the worst they can do is foreclose on your property. But borrowing $500 to $1,000 from a blood relative is quite another! They can play with your head for years.

I got this scary premonition that normally affable Aunt Meg was going to turn loan shark on me and send some goon over with instructions to "do whatever they needed to do" to collect the debt. I conjured up frightening images of a cat's head in my bed, of Guido with the crooked nose holding me upside down by my feet and dangling me from some fifteen-story balcony, loose change falling from my inverted pockets in a menacing prelude to my fate on the ground below.

"Meg wants the money!" I could hear Guido yelling over my terrified screams and pleas for mercy. "I'll get it to her" were the words I envisioned. "I promise I will. What about all those times we went to church and went on vacation together? Doesn't that count for anything?"

"It's business," the tough guy countered in a raspy voice. "Nothing personal." Bastard.

I still hadn't quite recovered from the notion that, only four years prior, we had been forced to sell our cute little one-year-old Toyota station wagon because, due to our shaky financial situation, a monthly rent payment and a monthly car outlay simply couldn't coexist in our ridiculously tight budget. The sheer embarrassment of it all! But no matter, things were looking up. Life was generally good. We were healthy. We had a home. We had roots. We were on our way!

My favorite relaxation clothing at this juncture of my life consisted of an old sweatshirt (or T-shirt, depending on the season) and a pair of jeans. But these weren't just any jeans. They were made for me, or at least it seemed that way. I'm sure many of you have possessed an article of clothing or an eclectic hodgepodge ensemble that, for you, represented the ultimate in relaxation apparel. An old stand-by, a coveted outfit that you instinctively threw on when you wanted to clean the house or just get comfortable. A favorite sweat suit, perhaps, or an old bathrobe.

I'll even let you ladies in on a little secret. I know for a fact that there are a lot of men who are not only partial to a particular outfit but are uncommonly sentimental when it comes to their undergarments. Not only are we loath to the idea of stopping the car and asking for directions, but we men, for some reason, seem to grow very attached to our boxers and not-so-tighty whities, especially undershirts. We wear undershirts not just until they wear out but also until they practically *vaporize*. I personally hang onto my undershirts until I am strongly urged by some member of my immediate family to trash them. By this time, there is usually not enough material left to make a good dust rag.

I classify such attire as an ASD, an adult security blanket, like the bottle that my oldest daughter, Jaime, carried everywhere until she was about to enter kindergarten. Jaime would ask for, in order of preference, a bottle of milk, a bottle of juice, a bottle of Tang, or—fearing the worst—a bottle of cold water. Except she pronounced her final desperate request for juvenile liquid "bottle-a-cold wah-dare." Concerned that she might want to hold this beloved bottle in one hand and her wedding bouquet in the other, we eventually had to practice a tiny bit of deceit.

My wife and I were forced to hide her bottle and sadly break the news to her that it was "lost." Despite the fact that she is now married with a child of her own, she still holds us responsible to this day.

As I recall, I never wanted to launder my personal security blanket, the aforementioned comfy denims, because the washing and drying process made them stiff and took away that comfortable, broken-in feeling. So I continued to wear them until they became offensive and the offended party, usually my wife, shamed me into taking them off. "If you don't wash those jeans, they are going to stand up and walk by themselves" was her typical lame warning.

But even when badgered, I never acted hastily. Since I had never witnessed these jeans, or any other article of clothing for that matter, actually stand and take steps on their own, I tended to discount her theories, to brand them as pure hearsay. I thought long and hard before I subjected my favorite dungarees to the rigors of machine washing and drying.

My jeans and I were an item, a real pair. Nothing could separate us. If I could count on nothing else, I could count on them.

Then one day I came home from work and instinctively reached for my faithful Levi's. But as I slid them on, I began to encounter unexpected resistance in the vicinity of my buttocks.

I was perplexed. I had just worn these slacks the day before and had met no such opposition. What dramatic changes could have taken place in a scant twenty-four hours? I wrote the incident off as a one-day fluke and went on as if nothing had happened. Deep down, however, I knew something was amiss.

With each passing day, my confusion grew. What I had originally diagnosed as a one-time freak occurrence of nature had blossomed into an ugly fact of life. My beloved jeans had become ill-fitting. It didn't take a rocket scientist to figure out that either my favorite garment had morphed or I had. I didn't like either option. Still, I didn't panic. Instead, my keen analytical mind began to formulate a list of possibilities:

- **Possibility 1:** My wife switched my jeans with an identical pair a size smaller as her idea of a practical joke. **Conclusion:** An excellent prank. In fact, I would have to try it sometime—but not her style.
- **Possibility 2:** My new bodybuilding regimen had pumped up my legs and buns to the extent that they were now in competition for the limited space available. **Conclusion:** Not likely, since I hadn't altered my routine and, frankly, so macho a proposition that it made me a bit nauseous.
- **Possibility 3:** A sudden, unexplained weight gain. **Conclusion:** Not physically possible.
- **Possibility 4:** In the middle of the night, I had been abducted by aliens who had poked and probed my body for hours and then exposed my rear end to gamma radiation. **Conclusion:** I had read too many of those supermarket tabloid covers.

The results were inconclusive to say the least, leaving me with scant recourse. Yes, there was only one thing left for me to do. Feeling that the problem must lie with me, I did the unthinkable. I forced myself to stand in front of one of those ridiculously honest full-length mirrors, the ones that most of us avoid at all costs unless we happen to catch a glimpse of ourselves as we stroll past one in a department store.

Standing sideways with my pants around my ankles, I gasped in horror as I beheld the problem. Much to my amazement, my once-firm derriere had slid downward and had taken up residence on the area designated for my upper thighs. Translation: *My butt had fallen, and it couldn't get up!*

My first reaction was shock. My eyes were playing tricks on me, I thought. What manner of insidious disease, what form of unspeakable parasite could make a beloved body part collapse overnight? How could one section of the body encroach upon an area occupied by another? The mere thought of such an interaction seemed almost incestuous. I felt a strong urge to take a shower.

It took quite a while for me to truly grasp the reality of the situation. I now realized why younger women were able to shun the uncomfortable brassieres while their older counterparts seemed resigned to wearing them. Obviously, it had a lot to do with the firmness of their breasts. It was apparent that what may not require support in its youthful stages usually requires a considerable amount of support in its latter stages. In other words, what stays up must eventually come down. It also became apparent why women, as they advance in age, tend to wear less-revealing clothing and pay huge sums of money for facial surgery, tummy tucks, and extensive liposuction.

We males, meanwhile, seem to be under direct attack from Mother Nature herself, undergoing a metamorphosis that defies logic. To think that the run-of-the-mill nourishment that we guys ingest all of our lives with no apparent ill effects can suddenly become our mortal enemy is almost maniacal. Unable to be siphoned off for fuel as efficiently as it had been in our youth, these nutriments quietly begin to accumulate as fat cells on our post-forty frames. Then, to add insult to injury, the majority of these fatty malingerers tend to head straight for our midsections like a herd of migrating wildebeest.

Forgive the questionable metaphor, but if you've ever watched one of those nature programs and witnessed the wildebeests, tormented, totally instinct-driven, homely, four-hundred pound creatures swimming through rivers teeming with twenty-foot crocodiles simply because this body of water happens to be part of their migratory route, I'm sure you catch my drift.

Who devised these elaborate relocation patterns, this roadmap from hell, in the first place? The crocodiles would be my guess. The migratory instincts of the wildebeests are obviously much stronger than their will to survive. What manner of cruelty is this? Mother Nature, you back-stabbing diva, cut these poor devils some slack!

The wildebeest trek is such a well-known phenomenon that the monster reptiles are lying in wait, their beady eyes protruding from the water like evil little periscopes, watching and waiting as their meals arrive. They don't even have to leave home for it; it's like pizza delivery without having to tip the driver. I'm surprised they don't have dinner napkins wrapped around their necks and a knife in one hand and a fork in the other in anticipation.

In some cases, the normally stealthy amphibians—they're considered ambush predators—forsake the element of surprise, grow impatient, and actually leap from the water and pull the ugly wildebeests to their deaths. Many of those that manage to traverse the river of death end up being trampled by their comrades in the rush to exit as they climb the opposing riverbank to safety—an ignominious ending to say the least, adding insult to injury to an animal already encumbered with the body of a steer and the head of a lawnmower.

If I were one of these maligned creatures, I think I would have to call my motor club and have them work up an alternate route. If you think you have a tough life, you might want to consider the plight of the poor wildebeest.

Fighting the Effects of Gravity

But I digress. Our stomach muscles, meanwhile, which could always be counted on to hold the line in the past, cruelly desert us in our hour of need, allowing this new-formed girth to head for points south. Without putting up the least bit of resistance, without so much as a "look out below," these muscles-turned-traitors meekly succumb to the powerful forces of Ms. Nature. We're left in the lurch. Before we know it, our belts have been overrun, totally out-manned by the sudden surge.

The effect is one of a metabolic experiment gone terribly wrong. Without any sort of change in our diet or exercise regimen, our chest, waist, and hips eventually meld into one big, flabby eyesore, a stubborn preponderance hanging uncontested as if laughing at its host.

The whole process reminds me of one of those old Japanese monster movies with out-of-sync English voice tracks that I used to watch on Saturday afternoons—the movies that depict a dastardly scenario in which large doses of radiation wreak havoc on plants and wildlife. If you ever watched one of these sci-fi classics, you'll recall the pattern that always developed. As the film progressed, abnormally large but for the most part harmless creatures are spotted roaming throughout the countryside, an ominous sign of things to come.

Scientists are at a loss to explain what is happening. A large freighter—obviously a scaled-down, ridiculously phony imitation of said freighter placed in a small pool, but we didn't know the difference—loaded with a crew of grizzled seafarers is mysteriously attacked, their ship smashed in the ocean like an eggshell. The next thing you know, Godzilla is playing kick-the-can with Tokyo.

Some twisted souls had crossed the line—mindlessly thrown sand into the face of the world order—and things would never be the same. But I wasn't witnessing a fictitious account. This was no movie. I was staring into the face of middle age, and it wasn't a pretty sight. I shuddered at the implications.

The reality finally struck home. This shocking transformation was, in actuality, that middle-age condition that everyone talks about. Like a joke that had taken me years to catch, all the phrases that had gone in one ear and out the other throughout my lifetime were now starting to hit home: beer belly, gut, love handles, spare tire, shifting body weight, and the worst moniker of them all—middle-age spread!

Somehow the word got out. My friends and family began to joke about my predicament, telling me that Mr. Gravity had gotten the better of me. Obviously, choosing to bask in the misery-loves-company aspect of my situation, they took a certain pleasure in rubbing it in, giving me a taste of my own Mister medicine. "Damn that Mr. Gravity," they laughed, throwing my phrase back in my face. "Where's Mr. Stick, Daddy?" my oldest daughter said. "I guess he can't help you."

My wife took a different approach: "So your ass fell. I can't even tell the difference. Do you know what kind of problems women have with their behinds? Get a grip."

My father, whose rear has yet to give way, never drifting south so much as one centimeter, was especially brutal. Unable to relate to my condition, he still plays the cruel "butt card" for comic effect, making crude references about his son's condition for cheap laughs. "Heard your butt fell, huh? That's too bad. It happens to people at your age, though. I can get you some new pants if you need some. Tee-hee-hee." Thanks, Dad.

Meanwhile, I tried to keep up a game front. I pretended to laugh off their taunts and play down their insensitive ridicule. But, deep down, I feared the worst. Not only had the Mister pendulum begun to swing in my direction, but the realities of middle age

Fighting the Effects of Gravity

were hitting home like never before, pounding on my door like a landlord demanding an overdue rent check.

Suddenly, when I looked at gravity-ravaged men, it was like gazing into a crystal ball. It seemed inevitable that I, too, would one day have to face the music. There was no getting around it. My lot had been cast. Seemingly overnight, I had officially crossed over the line that separates the young from the not-so-young anymore. I was adrift in that vast middle ground of life, a card-carrying member of the middle-aged. I began to think differently about what we all learned in science about Sir Isaac Newton. It is very apparent that we have all been duped. We were told only of gravity's noble deeds. Clearly, they hid the evil from us. Yes, I know, the pull of gravity is what keeps us from flying into space, but it obviously has a dark side, too. Gravity's long-term effects on the human body can be pretty devastating. The bottom line seemed so unfair: even if you manage to live long enough to see middle age, you must stand by helplessly and watch as your body is pulled in all different directions.

By the time I reached the age of forty, my worst fears had come true. My own stomach muscles had started to slide, having begun their long, slow descent at age thirty-six.

But there was very little that I could do about it. Ironically, sit-ups, stomach crunches, and other alleged tummy-tightening maneuvers were for the most part ineffective—seemingly spinning their wheels against the onslaught. Unknowingly, my eating habits had become part of the problem. My caloric intake remained the same, but my metabolism—a new player in this game—had begun to slow down in a surreptitious manner. Damn you, Mr. Metabolism. But in my defense, there was certainly no Dr. Oz or *The Biggest Loser* TV shows to help me back then, no personal trainer to yell insults at me and work me until I vomited. How was I to know the score? The defiant muscles, meanwhile, in their new state, seemed unwilling to provide anything more than a nice, firm safety net for the orphaned abdomen.

Their prolonged departure was agonizing yet sentimental. After all, it isn't easy to watch a once-vital friend become complacent, to succumb to the reality that an always-dependable ally could no longer pull his weight. I was at least thankful that these muscles departed with some class, that their exodus was done in less dramatic fashion than that of my inconsiderate buttocks.

Make no mistake. His Honor, Mr. Gravity, had indeed covered all the bases. His jurisdiction obviously included negating the effects of extemporaneous exercise programs. The message was clear: "You can exercise until you're blue in the face, but your stomach is never going to be flat again. I will, however, afford you the luxury of this nice, firm carrying case."

Chapter 3: Oh, My Aching Body

ONE NIGHT DEBBIE AND I were having dinner with some friends, and when the evening had ended, we all stood up to leave—gathering our belongings—but remained huddled around our chairs. We continued to chat—mostly small talk—discussing the merits of the meal, all the while stretching our arms and legs about and twisting our trunks back and forth. But we all knew what was going on. It was a ruse. We were stalling. Stiff from two hours of sitting, we were all trying to get our sea legs—none of us apparently wanting to suffer the indignity of stumbling like toddlers in their first steps, looking like Tim Conway as the old man in the *Carol Burnett Show*.

We eventually looked at each other and smiled, knowing that we were all suffering from the same affliction. We were feeling the effects of the malady known as midlife. We were mentally enriched from our visit but physically stiff. Like a boxer who had just had his "bell rung," we needed a little time to shake loose the cobwebs.

We were all well versed in the new rules. Midlife had changed the game. The truth is we can no longer sit for hours while driving, attending sporting events, plays, movies, and dining out and then expect to just jump up and make a beeline for the exit like we're twenty. God help us should someone yell fire. The seventh-inning stretch in baseball should become an institution for the midlifer.

All events that require individuals to sit for long periods of time should have a time set aside for everyone to stand, walk about, and sing *Take Me Out to the Ballgame*. Sometimes I simply stand up during dinner and state the need to stretch my aching body—no shame in my game.

The whole adventure reminds me of a time at a local amusement park just a few years ago when my girls and I—I get in for half-price; age has its perks—made the mistake of getting on an indoor roller-coaster ride. Modern coasters are ominous enough when you can see them in the light of day; having yourself fastened into one without knowing your fate is just not a smart move.

While none of us agree on exactly what transpired on the ride, I felt a lot of spinning—which I avoid like the plague—typical roller-coaster ups and downs, and at least one upside-down loop. My daughters insist that there was no loop. When the ride ended and we could see the precious sun, we just sat there trying to get our heads clear, waiting for the earth to stop spinning, not one of us wanting to take the first step and fall on our face. The young girl operating the ride—she looked to be about twelve in midlife years—looked at us from her perch at the control booth and finally said, "You guys can leave now."

Middle age is the time in life when we begin to get those mysterious aches and pains from places that we never felt pain before. We make audible noises when we get up and sit down. The body begins to break down, slowly lose its momentum—like a car that is no longer under warranty and carries bumper stickers from two presidential campaigns ago with 50,000 miles on the odometer hoping to get to 100,000. Sometimes the bumper stickers are on the trunk and fender. That bugs me. They're bumper stickers, not trunk stickers. They'll stick to your paint. What are you going to do when you trade that car in?

You realize that the very same knee, elbow, hip, ankle joints, and lower back that treated you so well in your twenties are no longer your friends, that they no longer have your best interests at heart. They function, but they do so under duress, against their better judgment. Joints begin to ache; muscles follow suit;

Fighting the Effects of Gravity

backs can go awry when provoked. Pain becomes a constant companion.

Even getting up and sitting down can become an adventure. If you're anything like me, you no longer sit on soft, comfy living room furniture—you fall into it. The force of gravity pulls you into a chair as if someone had grabbed you by the back of the collar and yanked you there, often causing you to release an audible expulsion of air as you hit your target. You often feel the need to make some kind of statement as you hit. If you don't have one of your own try this one: "Oh, my goodness!" Say "Oh!" right at the moment of impact.

Rising from a cushy comfortable chair or couch, meanwhile, can be particularly brutal. Remember when you had the oomph to just jump right up from a low-seated position? Well, times have changed. Now you have that invisible force grabbing you by your midriff and pulling you back. Sometimes it takes me two cracks to get it right. I hit the apex of my climb and then tumble back into the chair. Then on the second try I rear back to gain some momentum and use it to reach the summit. Sometimes, a family member, friend, or polite stranger—if I'm not at home—will lend me a hand and pull me to safety. My rule of thumb is simple: if you sit low enough in a chair that coins drop from your pocket into the chair, you shouldn't be sitting in that chair.

And don't even think about flopping into those ridiculous bean-bag chairs. Who invented those things anyway? I consider them a padded extension of the floor. It's a long way down and a ridiculously awkward, unpleasant trip up. I see absolutely no way of getting out of that killer cushion without rolling over onto your knees and standing up from a kneeling position. You don't need that.

I won't go into the perils of lowering and raising oneself from a low toilet other than to say that there are elevated toilet seats and higher standing toilets available. Don't be put off by the fact that these apparatus are sometimes labeled as handicapped devices. Let's face it; we're all physically challenged at this point.

I've also found that getting out of a car can be a particularly difficult proposition: twisting one's body from a seated position behind a steering wheel, standing, putting all of your weight on one leg while rising all in one motion in a confined space isn't easy when you're middle-aged—especially when you consider that you're stepping into oncoming traffic. Hint: Grunt, try that expulsion of air thing, and keep an eye peeled for unsympathetic trucks and busses.

Oftentimes, old injuries incurred in our youth can come back to haunt us in midlife. Young bodies can be tricky. While they start off eager to please, don't be fooled—they're just biding their time for fifty years, plotting their revenge, waiting for the right moment to pounce. And they're no longer shy. They speak freely now. It's as if they have formed a union to protest the damage that has been perpetrated upon them in the past. They are tired, and they just won't take it anymore. No sir, they are no longer going to just sit idly by and allow you to pound on them.

I knew I had joints when I was younger, but it was different back then. Like every other part of my body, I took them for granted. I never paid much attention until I actually incurred an injury to a particular area—then I acknowledged their presence. I would say, "I hurt my ankle" or "I twisted my knee." I applied ice to the injured area—if I did anything at all—and then went right back into battle. I was young, so the joint usually responded quickly. I seldom heard from the injured party again, but little did I know it was marked for future demolition.

When I was a youngster of ten to twelve, I often jammed my fingers—many times a thumb—into the joint playing baseball or football, causing a lot of pain and swelling. We called it a "stoved" finger back then. I'm not sure if that term is used now. Unfortunately, due to the crude diagnostic techniques of my youth, the medical criteria for whether a finger was broken was if the digit could be moved; therefore, many a stoved finger was actually a broken finger.

Debbie tells me that she fell while ice skating when she was seven years old and broke her wrist. But because she could move her wrist her family insisted that it wasn't broken, and she had to sit in pain until the event was over. Fortunately, hospital emergency rooms don't subscribe to the "can you move the joint?" specialty of witchcraft medicine. They normally perform x-rays to determine the severity of the injury. Otherwise, trips to the emergency room would be faster and much less costly for insurers—"She can move it; send her home."

Between the ages of sixteen and thirty, I was an avid weightlifter. I bench pressed up to 300 pounds and squatted with weights of 325 or more with very little complaint from my shoulders, hips, and elbows. My knees did file a formal protest at one point. I also pulled a muscle or two along the way. Those were fun times. Boy, did I look impressive in a sleeveless T-shirt.

But all that has changed. I'm finding that many of the joints that have been stoved, broken, and twisted, including elbows and shoulders pushed to their breaking point during workouts, are now speaking to me. They're saying, "Remember that time you thought you were the Hulk and tried to pick up all that weight? Remember all of those stoved fingers? Remember all of that heavy bench pressing? Remember how you impressed your friends in the gym? Remember the times you worked out and didn't warm up? You looked really good for a while there, didn't you? Well, we're members of Local 280 Union of Muscles and Joints, and we're here to file a formal complaint. We cut you a break then, but now it's time to play hardball."

Steps can be a true mayhem for many midlifers—an absolutely brutal endeavor, the tools of the devil. My family's home is a three-story, twenty-room Victorian mansion that they purchased in the late sixties. This area of Pittsburgh is full of historical homes, many of which, like ours, were built before the turn of the century. One of the homes in the same block as ours features a "widow's walk"—a railed rooftop platform that, as the myth holds, allowed mariner's wives to watch for their spouses' return from sea. In truth, it is actually a decorative platform built on many nineteenth-century coastal homes.

When I was unmarried and still living at home, we fully utilized all three floors, my mother being the main culprit with her vast array of clothing. My mother had, at that time, and still has for that matter, a hook-up, an owner of an ultra-personal clothing shop—whom we shall call Suzanne—who provided her with elegant fabrics. Suzanne, ah yes, a name that conjures up visions of clothing days gone by, striking fear into the hearts of closets far and wide. Suzanne has become a household word in our home, practically a member of our family.

In their heyday in the seventies, my mother not only paid visits to Suzanne's emporium on Saturdays but received high-priced parcels by mail known as "care packages," to-die-for outfits that Suzanne knew my mother would not be able to resist. My mother would often hide these pricey containers under the bed, safe from my father's prying eyes, but she really did so solely for her own entertainment; my father could care less.

However, as the saying goes about weaving a tangled web, my father, on one fateful day, did happen to intercept a sizable invoice from Suzanne and almost fainted when he saw the bill, which was well into the thousands of dollars. My father, having seen the wizard behind the curtain, then knew the score. The game was over; the spell was broken. The Suzanne–Betty connection lives on, although at a much more humble level.

Unfortunately, large homes like my parents' require large amounts of stairs between floors; therefore, there are about fifty stairs that separate the first and third levels of the home. My parents lived on the first floor, my grandparents and I lived on the second floor, and third floor housed my workout area, a pool table, and the aforementioned walk-in closets and other storage rooms.

I can't help but remember how I laid claim to those stairs in my teens and early twenties, how I gave them no quarter, how they were mine, how I would brazenly run up those fifty stairs, two stairs at a time, without being winded. Over the years, my parents have remodeled the home, and they now live in one-half of the building while the other half is broken up into apartments.

Fighting the Effects of Gravity

Recently, Debbie and I allowed my middle daughter, Erin, to move into our home and we moved into—yes, that's right—the third-floor apartment.

Debbie has an iron deficiency and often lacks energy, so she stops at each landing—there are four of them—and catches her breath. I take each step on with a passion to prove I still have what it takes. If I'm really feelin' it, I'll sprint the last flight. Besides, I need the exercise. If the stairwell is hot, the wind quickly droops from my sails. "Oh, these steps," I find myself saying. Sometimes I walk all the way to the first floor only to discover that I forgot my keys. "Oh, shucks!" I believe is what I said the last time it happened.

We have to eat, but carrying groceries to the perch is not a pleasant experience. Shopping is tiring enough. Having returned home, we sit in the car parked at the curb in silence for a few seconds until one of us says, "I would pay someone to carry these packages up those steps." We do have a system. I tell my wife to bring the bags to the front door or to the first landing and I'll carry them up to heaven's doorstep. Who said chivalry is dead? I pay a visit to my chiropractor that week and cry on his shoulder about my back pain. "Anything that you may have done in particular?" he asks me. "Lift something heavy, carry groceries up those stairs?" It's an ongoing battle, but I'm up for the task. "You and me, steps," I say. "I've got something for you today."

Going down the stairs, meanwhile, is a totally different story. In my heyday, I would take on the stairs in a carefree jaunt, skipping down in full gallop without a thought for personal safety. Having fallen down flights of stairs on more than one occasion in the past few years, however—I was wearing slippers the last time—I have now acquired much more respect for the downward trek. I take them on one at a time. I take no step for granted, leave no landing unturned.

While I'll still carry my grandchildren up the stairs, I refuse to cart any live human cargo down a staircase. Standing at the top of a long flight of stairs and staring down, unable to grasp a banister while cradling an innocent child, feels like an Alfred

Hitchcock movie—*Vertigo* with the late, great Jimmy Stewart comes to mind. I see red flags; I hear John Williams's *Jaws* music. I figure that if I fall that's one thing, but there's no sense in taking someone down with me.

A set of gimpy knees and steps definitely don't mix. I'm always a little hesitant when I approach a set of stairs because I know that I'm going to feel pain from each knee upon impact. I no longer have the fluid motion that I used to have. Each step requires that body weight be placed on one rickety knee and then the other, causing each foot to hit hard with a flat thud.

In terms of running, I have a sixty-four-year-old acquaintance who travels the world to compete in track and field meets against men his age—genetic misfits all. Although I have never seen him race, him sprinting in a one- or two-hundred-yard race must bear a striking resemblance to an *X-Men* movie. As a middle-aged person who can barely navigate an uneven sidewalk—don't you hate it when your foot drags on uneven spots—I've decided that I really don't care for him very much. He's just way too athletic and genetically superior for his own good. Okay, so I'm jealous.

And as if all of this in-your-face, straight-shooting pain weren't enough, I have also noticed this slow-reacting muscle pain, pain that doesn't even have the decency to hit you right straight away, that waits for a couple of days to rear its ugly head. For instance, if I wash and wax my car on a Saturday, I may feel tired but otherwise have no overt symptoms to speak of. But two days later, on Monday, I develop this mysterious ache in my neck, shoulders, and arms. Because of the gap in time I have to go through this awkward process of elimination to figure out why my body is aching. "Oh yeah," I finally conclude, "I washed and waxed the car."

Why the two-day waiting period? I'm not buying a handgun. Is there no statute of limitations that governs the onset of suffering? Come now; either it hurts or it doesn't. It's as if the section of my brain that handles discomfort needs the extra time to process the pain.

Fighting the Effects of Gravity

I can visualize my overmatched brain cells handing out numbers to these various ailments, asking them to stand in line and be patient like customers at the supermarket deli counter, and then barking out the numbers. "Sixty-five? Sixty-six? Okay, when did he incur you again?"

Midlife joints have also formed an alliance in their quest for discomfort. They often team up with their buddy, arthritis, to make our lives more miserable. I had no idea how insidious an affliction arthritis was until I became a sufferer. Due to all of that wear and tear on the body, many midlifers suffer from an affliction known as osteoarthritis. Any time I hear of severe climate changes from warm to cold or cold to warm, I brace for the pain. I feel it in places that I didn't know I had joints. In addition to the big stuff—elbows, knees, shoulders, wrists—I feel aches and pain in the smallest joint at the tip of my pinkie finger. Pain radiates down my forearm. I can't imagine what rheumatoid arthritis sufferers have to go through. Some people even put a face on the arthritis disease, choosing to call it Arthur, but I'd rather not treat it like some kind of lingering friend. Arthritis is the one that makes me choke down all of the pain medication. I'll save the title of Arthur for the cute little alchoholic character made famous by Dudley Moore.

Sure, people, midlife can be a painful experience. It can leave you feeling down and out, like you've been tackled by a linebacker. Walking, standing, sitting, dressing, cleaning, and even getting out of bed can all lead to some discomfort. But what do you expect? You're 50 to 75 percent through this little exercise—of course you're going to develop some scars, feel some cumulative effects of a lifetime of hard knocks.

Still, I find that there's no need to just bite the bullet. Fight fire with fire—try a little hair of the dog. Lift some weights. Put some stress on those painful joints and stretch those stiff muscles. My mother, the ageless one, is eighty-two years old and—despite the fact that she has arthritic joints—has a physical trainer and exercises more than I do. She says she is willing to ignore some level of reasonable pain. My father—years removed from his athletic days and having endured two knee replacements—has chosen to run a sideline route. He drives my mother to her exercise sessions and watches her work out. But don't follow his lead. Keep on moving; don't let the pain get the better of you. Ignore the picket signs. Fight the union of muscles and joints.

Maybe one day, I'll fight the pain and get out there and start running sprints ... No, I'll just work on the steps for now.

Chapter 4: Middle-Age Sex

I MUST ADMIT THAT, since I have gotten older, my sex life has changed considerably. Yes, I'm finding that having descended into this valley known as midlife, sexual activity—although still enjoyable—is not quite what it used to be. Don't get me wrong, sex in midlife, if you play your cards right, can be even more pleasurable than it was in our youth. It just takes on a whole new look, a new dimension. Like everything else in middle age, sex is a bit more complicated, and it takes more planning. You just have to work at it a bit. I would have to say that, by the time you reach fifty, there are other items that have leapfrogged over your sex drive on the rungs of life and taken its place on the to-do list.

When my wife and I were younger—I was twenty-four and she was nineteen years old when we got married—sex was near the top of our personal to-do list. We were young; we had plenty of energy. Sex was like a new toy. We wanted to play with it every chance we got. Unfortunately, sexual novices that we were, neither of us knew what the heck we were doing. We knew what went where and who did what, but beyond that we were clueless.

As our relationship matured, our sexual relationship began to come of age as well. Sex became a more controlled, more thoughtful endeavor. And so it is in midlife. While youngsters might flail about in uncontrolled ardor, we midlifers tend to take a more direct approach. We have much more method to our madness. As our lives become more complicated, our sex lives become more complicated as well. While reaching sexual highs and screaming names and yelling out for one's deity is all well and good, when it comes to midlife sex there are often certain concessions to be made. We view matters in an entirely different light. Moral victories can become a reason to celebrate. Sometimes, partners just getting on the same page concerning a time and place is good reason to light up a cigarette.

It's been almost twenty years since a conservative banker type told me that he and his wife had pretty much roped off Friday night as their permanent home for sexual activity. Being a much more sexually aggressive creature back then than I am now, I found that notion to be a bit rigid and totally lacking in creativity. *Boy, that sounds like a good time,* I recall thinking sarcastically. *They're scheduling sex like a secretary contacts board members for a business meeting. Where's the spark?* I asked myself. *Where's the spontaneity?*

But now, in my late fifties, I am singing a different tune. Having one designated day per week for sex doesn't seem like a bad idea at all. That once-a-day, three-to-four-times-a-week gig was good while it lasted, but hey, I'm older, my back isn't what it used to be, and frankly, I just can't hang anymore. As Dr. Phil would say, "How's that workin' for you?"

And besides, I have more important things on my mind, like where I put my keys, whether my socks match, and how that next cold front is going to wreak havoc with my arthritis. I have bills to pay—the man calls me days, nights, weekends, and holidays for last month's car payment—thank God for caller ID. My Crohn's is acting up. I know what caffeine does to me; I shouldn't have had that iced tea at dinner. I'll work sex in when I get a chance.

Not to mention that, due to fatigue and husband-wife scheduling difficulties, impromptu morning free-for-alls have gone the way of the T. rex. The typical evening romp, meanwhile, often takes a backseat to a couple hours of TV, a snooze on the couch, and a drowsy stumble into the bed at midnight. All things considered, it will probably take the full seven days to guarantee a full recuperation. Yeah, give me a fortnight to rest little Jimmie Joe and I'm good to go—no apologies, no regrets.

But I also find that sufficient recovery is not the only positive. When it comes to sex in middle age, sometimes less is more—you have to pick your spots. You have to ask yourself, do I want one large hunk of pie tonight or three small, less-tasty pieces spaced throughout the week?

But sleep, yes, sleep I peg as the main culprit of the midlife sexual couple. Many a 10:00 p.m. appointment that my wife and I make is broken due to the demon slumber. I get caught up with some super-violent movie, chock-full of gratuitous sex, on cable in the living room and show up late to the party only to find my partner dead to the world—oops, my bad.

I slip back to the bedroom at the appointed hour and find my other half unresponsive; shame on her! I join my lovely in bed early with no appointment on a weeknight with larceny in my heart and she turns over and goes to sleep without so much as an *adios amigo*. I'll take the blame for that one too, but at least I tried. The message is clear: "You know I have to get up early in the morning. I don't even owe you an explanation."

Sometimes even when the contract has been signed, snoring can be heard during warm-ups. "You're asleep," my wife says.

"No I'm not," I plead on my behalf. More likely I was. At least we joke about it the next day: "Did something happen last night that I should be aware of?" I ask.

"No," she says, "not really."

But make no mistake, there will be no arguments or hassles—we're beyond that. This is the way we show our love. We're not anxious about our commitment; throughout our thirty-five years of marriage we have developed a bond that transcends sex.

The great thing is that midlife is a good time to get comfortable in your own sexual skin. With all of the myths, monsters, and legends out of the way, you can settle in and do what comes naturally. After all, there's nothing to prove. For me, the acrobatics are over. I'm not trying to impress anyone. There are no points for style, and no judges are going to critique me after the event.

God knows, if *American Idol* alum Simon Cowell were a fly on the wall I would be in deep doo-doo. Cue the British accent: "That was the most ridiculous display of human copulative activity I've ever seen!"

Gone are the gymnastics. I'm too old to hang from any chandeliers, not that I ever did before. I was never one for two-a-days. Braggadocio has left the building decades ago. If the whips, chains, handcuffs, Saran Wrap, and power saws are still in your arsenal, more power to you. But as for me, give me a well-planned date with the missionary or give me a good night's sleep.

I heard a man on the famed *Maury* show claim that he suspected his wife of cheating because their sex life was on the decline. Apparently, they had gone from having sex eight times a day to three times a day. While I will certainly give a nice long-distance high-five to this couple, I have to wonder if they have time for anything else. It also makes one wonder why there are no sexual events in the Olympics. I would have to think these two have a few gold medals coming.

If you're still looking for a good sexual home, consider the weekend a good time slot. Sex on a Saturday morning, for instance, can start the weekend off on a good note. But even this day isn't sacred. I have to consider the fact that there are grown children who own grandchildren who are up early on Saturday and who think that everyone is up early on Saturday. These children, even though they are all at or around thirty years old, also don't even want to think about the possibility that their parents might still be having any type of sexual contact. A ringing phone can be a bit of a turn-off. Remember when I spoke of careful planning? Put those cell phones on stun.

In terms of physical issues, I really can't complain. In fact, I feel pretty fortunate. Granted, my sexual apparatus doesn't function like it used to, but then again, neither does anything else. The important thing is that I have been spared some of the physical impairments that plague other midlife males. I have no need for Viagra, Cialis, or any other types of male-enhancement drugs, sparing me the horror of any "Oops, there it is" unplanned uprisings. I also worry about the side effects. I cringe when I hear that "If you have an erection that lasts longer than four hours ..." warning.

At times I find that there is some coaxing that must go on with both male and female parties. With menopause entering into the picture for the middle-aged woman and intermittent lack of willingness from the male end, patience is the password.

I can't help but marvel at the irony. I remember when I was a teenager how little it took for me to become aroused. Actually, arousal had nothing to do with it. Erections just showed up with little or no prompting. Blood rushed to that area like worker bees to their queen.

The little devil seemed to have a mind of its own. I couldn't control him. It didn't seem to matter if I was sitting in class working on an assignment or on a church pew singing hymns. I seemed to have no say-so, no choice in the matter. I certainly didn't need a *Playboy* magazine or a porno tape to get the job done—Mother Nature took care of everything. Apparently, she was running some unscheduled tests on the equipment; it was a dry run, a warm-up for the main event.

If the awakening occurred while I was sitting at my desk in class, I would nervously watch the clock, worrying that the bell would ring and I would be forced to walk to my next class in this awkward state. I could envision other students pointing at my genital area and snickering. Sure I could cover it up with my algebra book, but cut me a break—I wasn't in my right mind. Oh, if this predicament were of such paramount concern at my current age.

I often joke that my instrument was like a young combatant who was, when he came to attention with no prompting, in effect reporting to me like an eager recruit. "Private Robinson reporting for duty, sir!" he seemed to be saying. "Will you be needing me any time soon, sir? I just wanted to let you know that I'm ready for duty if called upon, sir!" There he was, all dressed up with nowhere to go.

"At ease," I would anxiously urge the novice. "As you were!" No wonder they say youth is wasted on the young.

These days, my once-enthusiastic enlistee still shows up, but he looks and acts a little differently now. These days he's a colonel. His hairline has shifted, I detect a bit of a pot belly, and he doesn't respond to commands quite as eagerly as he did in his youth. Sure, he falls down on the job once in a while, but he still gets the job done.

While very few of us guys used our organs for anything other than urinating back in my high school days, talk was king. Friends bragged about two- and three- and four-hour encounters when, in fact, the event—if there was one—probably ended before it got started. Back in the late sixties, my guess is that many a teenage plane never left the runway. But none of us really knew enough to burst anyone else's bubble.

In an obvious attempt at shock and awe, one of my high school buddies brought a Kama Sutra book of Hindu sexual enlightenment into social studies class for a project. It was the modern-day equivalent of a sixth grader bringing a loaded gun into class. We guys weren't terribly surprised at my buddy's lecture, because we had a chance to preview it before the presentation. I remember that the teacher was pretty cool about it, but she kept stopping him at various times when she thought he was getting carried away.

My best friend in high school developed a serious relationship with a girl from a suburban high school at the age of sixteen. I had the opportunity to spend a lot of time with them, and it was obvious even to me—naïve creature that I was, having never had such a relationship at this age—where they were headed. They struggled with the nature of their bond, their strong affection for one another at such a young age, and the fact that they considered premarital sex taboo.

Lest we not forget, these were different times; there was still a certain shyness and naïveté that doesn't exist now. There was still a raging controversy surrounding birth control pills. My friend's girlfriend couldn't just walk into a clinic as an unmarried female and be counseled like young girls can now. Guys still had to purchase condoms in a face-to-face manner at their local druggist. "Rubbers," as we called them, weren't sitting on the shelves at large chain supermarkets where you could slyly slip them to the cashier and hustle them into one of those blue plastic bags—not that I have ever done that. These days, condoms are passed out pro bono at some high schools like Snickers at Halloween.

My good buddy—to everyone's shock and amazement—came to school one Monday wearing a wedding band, having tied the knot over the weekend. As word spread throughout the school, we approached him at his locker to see the proof for ourselves. "Is (his new wife) pregnant?" someone asked. "Not yet," he blurted out, still trying to maintain some modicum of self-respect. Here was one of our own—a sixteen-year-old boy—showing up one day wearing a grown man's ceremonial ring. It was a marriage of inconvenience, with no invitations, no flowers, no honeymoon. The sudden nuptials seemed so out of place; it just didn't compute.

Sadly, he never really admitted that his new wife was carrying his child until she actually began to show signs of the pregnancy. I suspect the quickie marriage was a demand by the girl's father, made in a shotgun-style ultimatum.

But oddly enough, my friend became a Dr. Ruth, of sorts, for me and a few other male pals. While he never got into any intimate details of his own relationship, I recall him saying one thing that dispelled a lot of the teenage sexual myths. "I'll tell you one thing," he said in an almost mournful way, "don't believe what they say about that two-hour stuff."

This may make me sound like a real square, but one thing I can't understand about sex on TV and in the movies is the sweat. Why so much sweat? When it comes to sex, I don't like sweat. I'll work up a good sweat while I'm on a power walk, but I'm not too keen on it during sexual contact. Am I missing something? Is there something erotic about two sweaty human beings rubbing together during sexual contact? To each his own, I guess.

James Robinson Jr.

One of my all-time favorite movies is *Fatal Attraction,* which, as you may already know, features Michael Douglas as a cheating spouse and Glenn Close as his psycho mistress. The movie features several very erotic scenes, and when the two lovers get together for the first time they have a particularly wicked but sensual hook-up at Glenn's kitchen sink—complete with running water splashed about—followed by a slapstick, half-clothed tumble to her bed.

As they disengage from an obviously extended session they are dripping wet, not with moist little droplets but with a just-stepped-out-of-a-swimming-pool sweat. Okay, I admit it, I have watched this scene on several occasions, although never once have I condoned its prurient content. But am I to believe that, to be enjoyable, sex must be the equivalent of a triathlon? I guess one would consider this hot, steamy sex, with nothing before, nothing after, and just lots of sweating in between.

I suspect that, by middle age, we know better. By the time midlife rolls around we have learned that sex is not about sweat, it's about intimacy—quality and not quantity. In fact, it's not midlife sex at all; it's midlife love. We shouldn't have to sweat bullets to show how much we care. We just have to meet each other's needs and keep our bond solid. As we age, the goal is to keep sex on the radar, to keep it as a valuable part of our lives. While foreplay may be a foreign concept in our youth, it should become a valuable part our midlife experience.

I'm certainly not a sex therapist, but my advice to fellow midlifers is that if you're looking for a real turn-on, check out *Fatal Attraction* on DVD or cable; Blu-ray is a bonus. Keep an eye out for that elevator scene too, by the way. I have watched it once or twice. But make sure you turn off the movie before Glenn cooks the little girl's bunny; that's just wrong.

But if you want to be a part of a truly loving midlife relationship, consider a seven-day waiting period, set aside some time on your calendar, stay awake for the festivities, turn off the telephone, and try not to sweat. If you have to wear a sweat band, you're sweating too much. Yeah, lay low on the sweat. Otherwise, do whatever you like to do as often as you want. You'll be glad you did.

Chapter 5: The Agony of the Feet

THE SUBJECT OF FEET had always been a bit of a sticky wicket with my family. I remember my mother lamenting on a number of occasions that she was not blessed with a good arch, and for this reason, her feet were forever destined to be flat. She was often envious of my father and me, whom she looked up to as individuals endowed with exemplary arches. She used to make a point of proclaiming to me, in fact, that I had not just a nice arch but a "beautiful arch."

My father's feet, meanwhile, were practically the stuff of legends. His "great arches" belied the fact that his feet had taken a wicked beating during his days as a high school, college, and NFL football star. During a college game in the early forties at his alma mater, the University of Pittsburgh, he broke his left foot but continued to play in spite of the fracture. After receiving a shot of painkiller in the area of the break (yes, they did that even back in those days), he returned to the game and, remarkably, managed to catch a touchdown pass despite having to maneuver around on this tortured tootsie.

His damaged foot, however, never received proper medical attention and would never be the same. If anyone ever accidentally stepped on this tender area, he would limp around, wince, and moan until the pain subsided. I often joke with my father that he also played without a helmet but with no apparent harm done.

However, although my father's feet were suspect, the rest of his body was in pretty good shape even as he drifted into his midlife years. He's eighty-three years old today. He had what I like to refer to as one of those athlete's bodies. It wasn't that he was particularly muscular or strong in his post-playing years; in fact, he never ran or walked or did anything in particular to keep himself fit. He didn't have to. He could just do whatever he wanted when it came to athletics.

Jimmie Joe, as he was known in his hometown of Connellsville, Pennsylvania, and the University of Pittsburgh, was absolutely disgusting in his early thirties when it came to casual games of pool, volleyball, badminton, ping-pong, and softball. I say disgusting because if there was any trait of his that I could have really used it was his penchant for athletics and competitiveness. I was somehow bestowed with the passive, nonathletic, studious genes of my parents. While there is nothing wrong with inheriting all the scraps, these traits never came in very handy in a dog fight. It was as if a couple of sinister genealogists got funky and strung together some strands of DNA, laughing as they went. "Let's make this guy a pansy," they chortled.

One time at one of his Presbyterian summer retreats, my father, at the age of thirty-two, singlehandedly rescued a team of older camp staff who were being thrashed at a game of volleyball by a group of upstart counselors. The food at the camp was excellent, but the kitchen staff could really butcher a simple game involving a ball and a net. A two-zip match deficit quickly evened to two apiece due to his athletic prowess. The match was eventually called a draw.

And he always seemed quite humble and even embarrassed about the whole thing. No finger pointing, braggadocio, or trash talking. I never saw him attempt lacrosse, tennis, cricket, or Twister in his heyday, but I'm sure he would have quickly mastered all four.

My late grandmother's feet, meanwhile, were truly unique—two of a kind—straight out of the *Guinness World Records*. Her baby toes on both feet sat on top of her neighboring fourth toes

Fighting the Effects of Gravity

like some species of baby animal clinging to its mother's back. She never offered an explanation for this toe-hitching-a-ride-on-its-bordering-toe phenomenon. Perhaps she never wore the correct type of shoes for her feet, or perhaps her shoes were ill-fitting as a child. At any rate, this is a characteristic that I have never encountered on any other set of feet. I remember referring to them as "piggyback toes."

Yes, the foot issue was a real sore spot in my family, but as far as I knew, no family member—or anyone else who I had encountered, for that matter—had ever experienced what I would suffer through when gravity drew a bead on my forty-one-year-old feet. Suffice it to say that those "beautiful arches" my mother spoke so highly of would take a big hit. Here's the story:

The foot hysteria all began in my forty-first year. I was still reeling from the array of sudden changes in my physical appearance—the wilting posterior, the orphaned stomach, the gimpy knees, and other turncoat joints—when I began to notice an unusual aching in both feet. Since aches and pains had become an integral part of my existence, I simply wrote it off as yet another sore appendage. However, had I been a little more intuitive, I would have realized that my arches were screaming for help.

You would think that I would have acquired a sixth sense for this type of thing. However, I didn't really understand the true nature of the emergency until all of my shoes were fitting quite snugly. Once again, I failed to heed the warning signs.

Still in the dark, I headed to the shoe store. After a brief consultation with the salesman, I had to suffer the indignity of placing my middle-aged foot in one of those archaic foot-measuring devices usually reserved for children. It's hard to describe the strange feeling that hit me as I placed my foot onto this device again. I felt eerily out of place, like a fifty-year-old man going into a McDonald's restaurant and ordering a Happy Meal. Older individuals, it had always been my experience, could take solace in the fact that their shoe size would remain relatively constant. My feet obviously hadn't been apprised of this rule.

Nonetheless, this event proved to be quite nostalgic. Although I had never really learned the proper name for this appliance, our paths had crossed on many occasions. (I suspected that I would stumble upon the origins of this contraption while one day perusing the dictionary, just as I had happened upon the correct name for the Prussian army helmet—the *Pickelhaube*, as it turns out. You know, the one with the spike sticking out of the top. I was surprised to discover that the spike was actually used as a holder for horsehair plume when soldiers were in full dress.)

I had developed a close bond with the foot-measuring apparatus, which I have since come to discover is known as the "Brannock Device," in my youth when my feet were still growing and got reacquainted when my children's feet began to blossom at an alarming rate. But I was content with our current relationship, admiring the odd-looking contrivance from afar while my three children, whose foot growth had slowed to a reasonable level, were getting measured for $300 worth of the latest Michael Jordan offerings. My shoe size had remained consistent for the preceding twenty years, and I preferred it that way. I had a sizable amount of money invested in my current shoe collection. I definitely wasn't getting a real charge out of this reunion.

When my old friend, Mr. Brannock, the shoe-measuring device, broke the news that my feet had widened significantly, I was not really alarmed. The salesman even sought to reassure me. "Sometimes your feet get a little longer and wider as you get older," he said. His gentle words seemed to temporarily ease the pain. I started my new shoe collection without complaint by purchasing three new pairs and didn't even bemoan the fact that the manufacturer made special mention of the width.

However, when this new and improved footwear also began to feel a bit snug, I knew that there was something much more serious afoot than a little spreading of the feet. As a wave of paranoia overtook me, tiny beads of nervous perspiration began to blanket my middle-aged brow. I had obviously interrupted my arches in the middle stages of some skullduggery, secretly planning a terrorist act. Hatching a nefarious plot, they had apparently lain low until I had invested in more foot coverings and then cruelly let their intentions be known. Inconsiderate, yes, but I was getting used to that.

Once again, the reality of the situation swept over me. My head was spinning with the latest developments when the term "fallen arches" hit me like a lightning bolt. I put two and two together again, but this time the correct answer came like an urgent news flash: "Arches Fall, Gravity to Blame. News at 11!"

Not only were my feet taking a beating, but my virtue would even suffer. The demoralizing effects of these events would even pervade my normally unwavering sense of integrity. With a healthy dose of larceny in my heart, I returned a second round of footwear and attempted to convince the shoe salesman that he had sold me an ill-fitting pair of shoes. (I believe that my exact words were "What's going on here? Why would you sell me a pair of shoes that don't fit!")

But another consult with my honest pal, Mr. Brannock—who seemed to be laughing at me now—told a different story. I was embarrassed to discover that my feet had flattened to the point where only a few shoe manufacturers could meet my demands. I felt like a Jenny Craig ad in reverse. Before: 11-1/2 D. After: 12 EEEE. Were it not for the thoughtful people at New Balance, a shoe company that manufactures various styles of casual shoes in such widths, I would be forever destined to walk the earth in stuffy wing-tips and oxfords. Nike and Reebok are simply not in the ball game. How about this for a New Balance ad slogan? "New Balance: Shoes to fit the flat-footed, middle-aged man."

The store exchanged these "slightly worn" shoes for even bigger new ones, although the salesman poked holes in my indignant little charade. He took a quick look at the bottoms of my rejects, saw that they were considerably worn, and suggested that I might want to "wear the shoes around the house for a while in the unlikely event that they don't fit."

I have since discovered several artificial means of support for the archless foot, including foam insoles and heavy-duty arch supports, which I use in lieu of the flimsy foam braces provided by the manufacturer. This process usually involves removing the manufacturer's poor excuse for an insole, cutting off the toe section, and using the toe piece to supplement my store-bought arches—a complicated but necessary procedure.

Even after this process, the shoes take a little getting used to at first. I walk around the house in them for a while, but there's no simulating walking around outdoors in your new shoes performing your daily tasks: getting in and out of your car, walking distances, standing in grocery lines, tripping over curbs, running frantically after a bus. Eventually, I have to bite the bullet and venture from the pristine carpeted floors of my home to the cruel dirt, gravel, and concrete of the mean streets, which means, essentially, that I own the shoes no matter what they feel like by the end of the first day.

My left foot—the good foot—always goes along with the program. But the right foot, the larger of the two, is the troublemaker. The right foot often bullies the left into rejecting a new pair of shoes. If the delinquent refuses to be supported by my arch supplement, I'll feel my small toe on this foot rub against the top of the shoe, and I am, in effect, screwed—the transformation of the new shoe has failed. Returning the shoes will be all but impossible.

The situation reminds me of two young children, one well behaved, one, uh, "troubled." The parents, perhaps not knowing any better, might ask the troubled youth, "Why can't you be more like your brother?" Similarly, my rogue right foot would care less if I chastised it in such a manner. Most likely, I would receive the following reply: "You're not the boss of me."

Chapter 6: They Call It Presbyopia, but It's Still a Pair of Bifocals to Me

It's yet another telltale sign of the aging process—the one physical manifestation that touches practically every midlifer. It's the time when our vision begins to betray us, when we begin to go through all types of gyrations in an attempt to read the printed word. It's the time when we can be seen holding a newspaper or other reading materials at arm's length in a frustrated attempt to decipher the print when we take off whatever conventional eyewear we may be wearing to read something up close.

No, we don't need an arm extender; we need some type of middle-age eye correction—most likely bifocals. The message is clear: it's going to take an effort to read from now on, and you may look pretty stupid in the process.

It's what's known as presbyopia—loss of accommodation. It's the inability of the eye to adjust to see objects at different distances. But attaching a clinical name to it doesn't help when you can't read the funnies. Let's face it; it's yet another sign of our mortality.

For me, this piece of information was certainly no revelation. I could, in fact, see it coming from miles away. With body parts dropping all around me, I was informed, at age forty-two by eye professionals, that the time for bifocals had arrived.

Besides, it's not like I had perfect vision all my life. I got fitted for glasses before I hit puberty. With each trip to the eye doctor my eyesight worsened by leaps and bounds. My glasses became a virtual extension of my face—a plastic, functional, nonmalignant growth protruding from my ears and nose. I'm one of those people whom friends and family labeled as "blind." While I didn't require the services of a cane or a dog, it was really quite imperative that I wear glasses at all times.

My mother pointed this fact out to me and anyone else who would listen, quite often: "Oh, my God, he doesn't have his glasses. Someone get his glasses. He can't see." Thanks, Mom.

"When he gets up in the morning," she still emphasizes to a stranger, "he puts on his glasses first and then goes to the bathroom." Absolutely not the case, but I let her have her moment. In truth, even the blind can find their way around their own home, and I can maneuver about quite well in my surroundings even in pitch dark to empty my bladder. Going without corrective eyewear for extended periods of time, even in daylight or while driving, is a different matter.

The degenerative optical carnage eventually ceased as I got older, and in recent years my vision has actually improved. It's something to do with the elasticity of the eye—presbyopia in reverse. Some things really do improve with age.

When it comes time to take corrective action, I do, however, resent the control that eye doctors exert over extremely vulnerable middle-aged patients. Perhaps you haven't noticed, but when they swing that "Star Wars" lens manipulator-light-saber-diagnostic monstrosity in front of your face, it can have an almost surreal effect. I feel as if I have been transported to the land of virtual reality.

Then, for their next act, these supreme beings assume a role of absolute omnipotence by sliding the magical lens into position that enables their subjects to see fine print again. My own situation was magical. I could have sworn that I heard myself say, "O-o-o-o-h, a-a-a-a-h, there is a God!"

Fighting the Effects of Gravity

There is one scary moment, though, just before the magical lens is put into place when I can hardly read anything on the eye chart. You know, the Snellen chart, the chart on the wall with the huge letter E at the top representing 20/200 and rows of letters below, increasing one letter a line and gradually shrinking in size to the ideal 20/20. I think Snellen put that E at the top to make people like me feel better. "Surely you can see this one," Snellen, the Dutch ophthalmologist, must have scoffed. I'm not sure who is supposed to read those tiny specks of letters at the bottom. It reaffirms just how bad my vision really is. I feel so vulnerable.

I figure that if a Somali pirate held a gun to my head at this moment and ordered me to read some list of demands on that wall I would have to ask for larger script or suffer the consequences. I could hear my mother yelling, "He doesn't have his glasses! For God's sake someone get his glasses! He can't see without his glasses!" Thanks again, Mom.

Being as vain as the next person, one of my worries was that, with my having secured my bifocals, casual observers would immediately be able to spot my deficiency and would, without so much as knowing my name, have a large chunk of my personal life at their disposal. While I can conceal muscle aches, a falling derriere, and uncooperative sexual organs, there was no hiding this infirmity. Yes, one casual glance and it would be all over. Any Tom, Dick, or Harry with prying eyes would be able to ascertain that I had reached my middle years. They could easily spot that thick segment of magnification sitting at the bottom of each lens like a jeweler's eyepiece. And worse, they would be able to see me in the worst possible light, making the dreaded middle-aged face. More about this abomination later.

Call me radical, but the way I see it, bifocals are a visible sign of digression, a silent edict to all that the wearer has joined the midlife fraternity. Yes, I can't help but consider these sly little magnifiers as an invasion of privacy, an unsolicited testimony to all, loudly proclaiming, "Hey, look everybody. I'm forty-five years old!"

However, my worst nightmare was that one day, while innocently poring over some reading materials or gazing at a computer monitor, I would suddenly realize that my mouth and nose were contorted in a horrendous fashion. I would, no doubt, catch myself and look around to see if anyone had noticed. Yes, my worst fear would have then come to pass. I would have been guilty of striking that all-too-familiar pose, assuming the ridiculously unattractive "MAF," also known as "middle-aged face."

Having studied the reading styles of individuals middle-aged and up for quite some time, I became keenly aware of this particularly bizarre reading characteristic. I noticed that older individuals had a totally different reading style than their younger counterparts. Eventually, I traced this problem to the dreaded enemy of the middle-ager—the evil bifocal.

Due to the presence of this insidious but necessary little vision accentuator, we middle-agers are being forced to look like idiots just for the sake of reading printed material. It seems as if we are unable to decipher the language unless our heads are tilted backward at an obscene angle, our mouths are slightly agape (upper teeth exposed), and our noses are wrinkled as if a bad odor were present.

Perhaps driven by my mother's fateful warning about the dangers of continued facial contortions ("One day your face is going to stay like that"), I vowed that I would never distort my precious visage in such a manner. I would eschew the printed word altogether if that's what it took.

But compromise would save the day. I solved the vanity problem with a pair of glasses that, despite the fact that they contained the dreaded bifocal prescription, didn't have a telltale line to give them away—no-line bifocals, to be precise—and I paid through the bridge of my nose for the privilege. I have also been in touch with a host of other middle-agers who have chosen the "no-line" look, preferring not to publicize the fact that they require bifocals or even trifocals. Chances are that you too are exercising your right to corrective visual privacy. To those of you

Fighting the Effects of Gravity

who have aligned yourselves with this close-knit fraternity, I say, "Bravo!"

I also must confess, however, that I envy those of you who, despite being of the middle-age persuasion, have never required full-time corrective lenses. My father is of this ilk. You people have never had your glasses broken when hit full flush in the face with a basketball in gym class or had to suffer the indignity of wearing those clip-on sunglasses. Your eyewear has never dug in to the top of your ears and the bridge of your nose during the break-in period when you first purchased a new pair—oh, the pain—and you've never had anyone refer to you as "four eyes."

But even you fortunate souls have your Achilles heel. Consider a trip to a restaurant for instance. While everything may be fine and dandy while sitting at a table placing your drink order, terror awaits. Yes, everything is just hunky-dory until you have to … read the menu. Ha! Busted! That's when the reading glasses come out, your face takes on a whole new look, and the world knows the truth—you're middle-aged. And while you may not need glasses to see a hummingbird two miles away, you can no longer see fine print right in front of your face without assistance. Who could forget the mantra of the middle-aged reading-glass fraternity: "I can't read that. I need my glasses."

You're really waltzing to your own tune—laughing in the face of middle-age ridicule—if you choose to wear those half glasses that practically dare you to peer over top of the rims to jockey back and forth between close and long distance. And boy are you throwing all caution to the wind when you attach those straps and flexible cords to your glasses so that they can hang around your neck.

However, I really do admire the fact that nonprescription reading glasses can be purchased at any Wal-Mart, thrown right in the same shopping cart with the lunch meat and Mini-Wheats. It just doesn't seem right. You should have to spend some quality time with the *Star Wars* monstrosity like everyone else.

I'll never forget the first time I saw William Shatner's Captain Kirk *Star Trek* character standing on the bridge of the Starship

Enterprise wearing reading glasses. In this case, a picture definitely conveyed a thousand words. Just one piece of eyewear was all that was necessary to indicate that even Captain Kirk had succumbed to his mortality, surrendered to the inevitability of middle age. I can pretty much guarantee that Jim Kirk's glasses were not purchased at the local Wal-Mart and that he would not be caught dead making the insidious MAF.

But whatever situation you may be in, I must inform you that bifocals and reading glasses with cords won't do it alone. Know that the fiend presbyopia will rule our visual acuity until old age. Fine print will continue to be the enemy of the middle-ager. The only thing that you can do is roll with the punches. Do whatever makes things more comfortable for you. Find more efficient eyewear. Use better illumination. Just don't be caught squinting, taking your glasses off, and putting them on again—there's no need, and you'll make all of us look bad.

Bottom line: I want to see in comfort. I buy prescription sunglasses with no-line bifocals. I purchased a Bible with large print from Sam's Club to make my life easier. Sure it seems to weigh as much as the original Ten Commandments tablets, but heft be damned. I have a couple of good friends my age who actually pull out a magnifying glass when the need arises—now that really sucks. But whatever you do, don't dismay. Just be glad that you have the ability to see.

As for the possibility of falling prey to the twisted demon known as the MAF, I can only advise that you try to stay alert while reading. Remain conscious of those times that you are vulnerable to the lure of the middle-aged face. Yes, be aware, people; you don't have to look like this! You might consider this a hollow victory, but these days, I say accept victories no matter in what shape or form they may come.

Chapter 7: What's Up, Doc?

MIDLIFE DOCTORS—THERE ARE JUST too many of them. They come in all sexes, sizes, colors, and nationalities. I have a gastroenterologist, a primary care physician (PCP), a chiropractor, a cardiologist, a urologist, a dentist, an optometrist, and a psychologist. When I get to the next level, there'll be a doctor of geriatric medicine waiting in the wings to usher me to the promised land. I used to have a dermatologist, but after a certain point there was really nothing more he could do for me. Not to mention the fact that I outlived him.

When I was first pulled from the womb, I was immediately and quite informally introduced to my first doctor—an OB/GYN—whose duties were immediately assumed by a pediatrician. Then at the proper age, I segued to one doctor—known as a family doctor—who would handle my medical needs all the way until the early eighties. It was at this time that I matriculated into our massive clinical health system like a small fish into a sea of millions of other fish with varying degrees of health issues.

Practically everyone in my extended family saw our family doctor, Dr. Williams—now deceased—who became an iconic and very trusted figure to our clan. I saw him for every medical problem I had from acne to constipation. It was a sad day whenever he had to refer me out of his care into the care of another physician. Granted, I was a healthy guy back then, but this one doctor handled my every medical need.

In fact, I was his patient for so long that I got to know his ways. When I was sitting on the examination table and Dr. Williams turned his back to me and rustled around in a particular drawer where there were tiny instruments making tiny little instrument sounds, I knew what was coming—a cyst was about to be lanced, a prostate was about to be probed, an infected finger was about to be pierced with blood shooting throughout the room. I called it "the pain drawer." Finally, a family member squealed on me. During a visit, the doctor went to his trusty drawer and said, much to my chagrin, "What do you call this, the pain drawer?"

Family doctors back in the day—even before my time—actually made house calls. You remained at home and the doctor came and treated you in the comfort of your own bed with no nurse to supervise the visit; such was the trust factor. While this notion might sound preposterous now, medicine was very informal back then. There was no skyrocketing malpractice insurance and there were no lawyers prompting patients to sue the pants off of everything that moved, building a practice designed to make a living off of someone else's mistakes.

Back in 1996 at the age of forty-three, I had surgery for Crohn's disease, an inflammatory bowel ailment, which was late in being diagnosed and therefore required extensive surgery. As I lay on the gurney at 8:00 a.m., prepped for surgery, having come to grips with my mortality and calmly awaiting my fate, I looked around at the medical talent around me—a veritable who's who of the medical world. Hovering around me was a urologist—as "fistulas" from my intestines had allowed excrement to enter the bladder—a gastroenterological surgeon, an internist, and a few selected hospital interns, not-quite-physician groupies looking for a good time. In one of his early comedy albums, Bill Cosby, while he was waiting to have his tonsils removed as a kid, yelled at one of these young medical people walking by his room: "Hey you, almost a doctor!"

Fighting the Effects of Gravity

As I lay there trying to maintain my cool demeanor, I remember one of these twenty-year-olds—at least he looked that old—interns saying to me excitedly, "This is going to be a tough surgery." I forgave him for his poor gurney-side manner and the fact that he wasn't considering my needs. He was all geeked up for the show. After all, a real doctor had allowed him to watch my intestines being taken apart and put back together again.

When I awoke at 11:00 p.m., thirteen hours later, in intensive care with a funky heartbeat, tubes coming from every orifice, and my wife talking to a nursing friend of hers from college, I had to admit it. The brat was right. However, this ordeal didn't stop my nurses from pulling me from my bed the next day and forcing me to stand and take steps. I know the importance of getting out of bed as soon as possible, but I felt like I was being dragged to my death. The room was spinning in an ungodly fashion. I practically rued the day I was born.

The nurses showed up at my room faithfully twice a day to get me up and make me walk. I hated to see them show up at my bedside. Unfortunately, I had no choice but to go along with the program. There was nowhere to hide, and I'm sure they would have refused any type of payoff along the lines of "I'll give you fifty bucks if you let me stay in bed." It's amazing how hard it is to move about after this type of surgery—five steps feel like fifty.

During my seven-day stay, I watched as every tube was gradually removed from my body except the catheter. That invasive piece of hose went home with me and stayed in place with a urinary bag for another two weeks. One last trip to the urologist ended the ordeal.

While I certainly shouldn't complain, all of this specialized medicine can lead to certain problems. When I was a member of Health America back in the mid- to late eighties and early nineties, I was, for the most part, a healthy specimen. When I scheduled a visit, my PCP came into the examining room, we exchanged greetings, I discussed my problem with him, and he performed a perfunctory exam and wrote scripts when called for.

After that, I was usually speaking to his back as he was leaving the office. Duty called.

But in the middle years, thorough, meticulous physicians and specialists pose a different threat. As you grow older, they don't go flying out the door to get to the next patient. They spend quality time with you. You get to know them. They have a vested interest in your survival. Now that I'm about to cross the sixty-year threshold, they don't consider me young anymore. During one office visit, a particularly thorough PCP noticed a problem and sent me directly to the hospital. "If you were twenty-eight or so I wouldn't worry," she said, "but at your age I don't want to take any chances." Yeah, I know, it's called erring on the side of caution. But I call it scaring me to death for no good reason.

Now when I see my cardiologist for a six-month checkup I keep my middle-aged trap shut about little aches and pains that may be in the vicinity of the heart area. If I make any mention of a slight pain in my upper chest near my shoulder, I'll be eating tasteless baked chicken in the cardiac unit before you can say, "But I really don't think that it's anything heart related." I know that this isn't the proper attitude, but I'll have to feel the equivalent of an elephant on my chest before I mention such a symptom to him. I love you, Doc, but you worry too much.

Having so many physicians means a good chance of copious amounts of the finest medication that drug plans and Medicare Part D can buy. I take six pills a day for various ailments—hypertension, migraines, anxiety, and mood control ("crazy" as my wife refers to it). I also ingest eight capsules per day for Crohn's disease alone. Then on top of that I throw in a healthy dose of over-the-counter drugs like ibuprofen, acetaminophen, and naproxen for my aching back, joints, and bones—I mix and match. Medication available to us as part of our prescription plans and generics at low prices are a godsend, but sometimes it becomes obvious that we are overmedicating.

Having so many doctors also guarantees that you'll get more than your fair share of those routine exams. Once you reach fifty or so, in fact, those "routine" procedures become quite routine. As a married man and co-producer of three young women, I can tell you that women consider their exams to be the most invasive and painful on earth. All of the women in my life have told me in great detail about yearly visits to their gynecologists. They go on about lying on an examining table wearing only socks with their feet in the stirrups, retractors in place; about how the doctor examines the patient like a coal miner digging away at a hunk of anthracite with his pick, all the while making small talk: "How have you been?" "How's the job?" "Your sister was in the other day."

Then there's the mammogram. "How would you like to have your breast smashed between two plates of glass?" they whine. Let's not even go into childbirth. I don't think you women will be happy until every man has had at least one child—dream on.

As a male, I can tell you that I've never met a man who even wants to discuss the yearly prostate exam. In fact, this exam is so despised that there are those fickle males who refuse to have it performed. I have never quite understood this mentality. While it certainly isn't a comfortable test to go through, the discomfort need only be tolerated for thirty seconds or less, and this is one exam that can save your life.

Believe me, gentlemen, I understand. The snap of that latex glove is a horrible sound. It sends chills down the spine of the most masculine of our species. But it's all a part of the process, a necessary evil if there ever was one.

If you think the regular prostate exam is bad, listen to this: I have been through an exam called prostatic massage in which the prostate is actually massaged until semen is released. The semen is then tested and analyzed for infection. Now that's one test I could do without. I plan on avoiding that one in the future.

A colonoscopy, meanwhile, is a different story. Once you reach fifty, depending on family history, you can look forward to these ordeals at least once every five years. My father is eighty-four, and despite the fact that he has had prostate cancer, he is no longer required to partake of any of these procedures. I find this development to be profoundly bittersweet. I'm sure he's grateful for the reprieve, but on the other hand, in what medical category would one place this decision? Is this considered the "Oh, why bother" school of medical thought?

Unlike the prostate exam for men, the colonoscopy is a widely discussed procedure among my friends and family. Everyone I have ever spoken to has agreed that the prep for the exam is far worse than the exam itself—which is understandable, seeing as the prep lasts twelve hours and the test takes about forty-five minutes. Indeed, having to clean one's entire bowel of waste and debris is a monumental task.

I often get into discussions with other midlife colonoscopy victims—boy, we midlifers are a boring lot—over which cleansing agent is best, or worst depending on how you look at it. Most agree that having to ingest the infamous Golytely—the gallon-size jug of glycol-electrolyte solution—in the time allotted is worse than eating ten pounds of prunes. We all make faces during the discussion and talk about the best techniques and strategies for getting this entire container of liquid laxative into one's system with as little notification to the gag reflex as possible. My sister-in-law—Mi-Mi, as she is known—has cleverly recycled an empty Golytely container and uses it to hold ice tea and other beverages. Now that's a true, real example of taking something bitter and making it sweet.

I want to come clean at this point and say that there have been times when I have intentionally left some of the solution in the bottle and simply refused to finish. I'm sorry. I just couldn't drink it all. May God have mercy on my soul.

But the bottom line is that we all manage to survive the prep and the ensuing test with very few side effects. After one day of bowel discomfort, the test is administered the following day under sedation. With the triumvirate of pain and sedation medication provided to me, I haven't remembered the details of a procedure yet. Following the last scope, the attending nurse actually had to wake me up. Ah, the wonders of modern-day sedation. The most memorable event on procedure day is getting the intravenous fluids flowing. The nurse always sticks you with those famous last words: "Big pinch." When the medication begins to flow into my IV I always remember thinking, *I feel really funny. I should tell someone. Naw.*

However, whatever it takes to get the job done, there is no excuse not to have this test or any other test done if it's in the interest of prolonging your life. The pain or discomfort is always minimal compared to the tests and treatment required for a serious illness. It all comes down to the question of how long you want to live. I have spoken to three individuals in my lifetime who have reached their sixties who admit they have never seen a doctor. Their reasoning has nothing to do with any religious beliefs but rather with a fear of death. They equate doctors to dying, perhaps associating some tragic occurrence to the medical community as a whole.

I agree that a hospital is not always the best place to be, but then again, allowing some illness or disease to go untreated just isn't rational. I believe that if you want to live as long a life as possible, then you take whatever measures you need to take and do what is best for you to achieve that goal. And if that includes drinking a gallon of nasty liquid once every three to five years and having digital exams in sensitive areas, then so be it, especially knowing that in 2007, over 143,000 people were diagnosed with both colon and rectal cancer combined and over 53,000 died from the diseases.

Besides, those of us with health coverage should be very thankful that we have access to all of the medical care and prescription drugs that keep us alive and well during our middle years. There are over fifty million Americans who have no health insurance in this country. I've seen the retail cost of some of my medication, and I don't know how I would pay for it.

So, come on, guys, that disgust and dread of someone performing a routine rectal exam for less than the time it takes you to a take two puffs of a cigarette has got to go. Grow up. And ladies, other than in the movies, we men aren't going to be having any babies any time soon, so get over it. Have your breast exams and mammograms performed on a routine basis and stop crying about it. Let's keep ourselves healthy and take our medicine like big boys and girls. Colonoscopies all around. Big pinch. Over and out.

SECTION TWO

Getting into the Middle-Aged Head

Chapter 8: I Can See a Little Too Clearly Now

*Life is as tedious as a twice-told tale
Vexing the dull ear of a drowsy man.*
William Shakespeare

HAVING TAKEN MY OLDEST daughter to college for her fall term in 2000, I happened upon a young bird sitting in the grass under a tree. This fluffy fledgling had obviously just been booted out of the nest as part of his maturation process. Do young birds come back home like our kids do? In his angelic state, he never saw the need to retreat to safety as I walked to within a few feet of him. On the contrary, he almost seemed to be smiling at me as I approached. He seemed to be saying, "Hi. I'm not sure where I am. Last thing I knew I was in a tree. Do you know where I'm supposed to go or what I'm supposed to do? Oh well, I'll just chill out here until I figure things out. Ciao."

My fine-feathered friend may have been free as a bird (sorry), but in his innocence he didn't have enough sense to fly away. I found myself getting anxious for his safety and warning him of impending danger. I think I said something like, "You're supposed to be terrified of me, you dummy!" He didn't heed my counsel, but I'm hopeful that he survived these early trusting days to become wary and cynical like all the rest of us. It does make one wonder how any young animal can survive long enough in the wild to reach adulthood.

I relate this story because, unlike my little fluffy friend, I feel as if midlife has placed me at the other end of the maturity spectrum. I'm observing many aspects of this existence clearly for the first time, like a nearsighted man who has just been fitted with a long-overdue pair of spectacles. It's as if, after watching the same play for half a century, someone has finally seen fit to lift the curtain. My philosophy these days could be summed up with a resounding "Oh, so that's how that works."

I would dare say that if I were the bird in question and someone were to approach me, not only would I fly away, I would probably flip them the bird—no pun intended—on the way up.

Yes, my body may be slipping, but my brain is definitely making up for lost time. Like those old transparent Invisible Man and Invisible Woman plastic replicas of the human body that afford one an uninhibited view of the male and female anatomy, I can suddenly see right through that crafty camouflage that had me snookered in my youth. I've got an unrestricted view of the proceedings. I'm observing this fellow Life in the raw, catching a glimpse of this shyster in his underwear.

Call me a late bloomer, but I actually feel more intelligent, more on top of things. I'm a lot more verbal and apt to speak my opinion than I was in my youth, more willing to express myself. No longer will professors say to me, "I wish you would talk more in class," like some of them did when I was but a soft-spoken young lad in college.

I'm also more of an individual. I have my own opinion, my own insight into others' behavior, my own set of values. I am more confident and more at peace with myself. I'm more likely to do what I want to do instead of what I think others want me to do.

Unfortunately, there is this one sizable catch, one formidable drawback to this intellectual resuscitation. Sometimes I think that the picture has become a little too clear. Maybe I've watched one too many gangster movies—seen Sonny Corleone meet his gory demise in the *Godfather* toll-booth scene one too many times—

Fighting the Effects of Gravity

but I can now sympathize with mobsters who knock off members of their own family simply for "knowing too much." I say, size me up for a cement overcoat, because at this point, I may be privy to just a little more than I care to be.

It seems that, though I have an extremely lucid picture of life, many of the sights that I'm observing aren't so pleasing to behold. Seeing life in all of its uncut, uncensored splendor means catching a glimpse of our being in some very unflattering poses. As you might expect, it's these negative angles that seem to attract all the paparazzi.

Like the antibiotics that were prescribed for me when I was a teenager that cleared up my stubborn case of acne but also provided me with a persistent dose of diarrhea, or the wonder drug that lowers a patient's blood pressure to acceptable levels only to diminish his sexual function to an *unacceptably* low level, some of the more unpleasant side effects of my mental upswing have surfaced. Apparently, this mental arousal has a noticeable downside.

For instance, it has suddenly dawned on me that, if I live long enough, I *will* get old. Yes, like it or not, old age is definitely in my future. It's also recently become clear to me that I'm mortal, that sooner or later, my physical self will cease to exist. Somehow, I never really took this death issue very seriously before. I may have been blind to these unattractive realities when I was younger, but unfortunately, I can see them with no annoying obstructions from this vantage point, halfway between birth and the everlasting.

Okay, I admit it. Having seen the rough spots, there are times when I entertain a notion of a return to simpler days, a retreat to life as I knew it, a time when the rules didn't seem to apply to me. Say what you will, but life was pretty simple then—sometimes not knowing can be blissful.

Think back to a time when you were oblivious to all of life's bitter pills, when you were unconscious to the cold, hard realities. Whether you knew it or not, you were a protected species then. You benefited from a kind of youth-sponsored safety zone. I'm guessing you were not only young but innocent, stupid, and pretty doggoned happy!

While still a resident of my own little la-la land, I considered myself akin to the Hindu sacred cow. During my early life and throughout my teenage years, distressing topics such as death, taxes, and the threat of nuclear holocaust seldom invaded my juvenile thoughts. I went to high school and studied, did lousy in math, went to parties, and stressed over females. My male friends and I had sleepovers—believe it or not—and watched a late-night Saturday horror show called *Chiller Theater* hosted by a Pittsburgh TV icon named Bill Cardille. At some point, Bill picked up the nickname of—get this—Chilly Billy Cardilly. The show started at 11:30 and played mostly "B" horror movies for most of the night. Don't forget, George Romero filmed *Night of the Living Dead*—one of the first super-gory horror films—in Pittsburgh. So the area was no stranger to the scary movie genre. Sure, we were lame, but it was a good kind of lame.

On one occasion, my lame friends and I went to a drive-in in my parents' car and two of them got in the trunk before we got to the pay booth and sneaked in without paying. Then the goofballs sang while awaiting release from their bondage until I found a spot to park the car. Oh sure, they had the money to get in, but that wasn't the point—it was simply for the fun of it. They were my best friends, and as I continued through school and moved into the meatier portions of my life, I've never found any friends quite like them.

Those were the days. I was gloriously out of touch, and this splendid situation didn't change much when I reached my twenties. I lived at home until I got married at twenty-four, and I was still pretty naïve about the world.

My parents and most of my close family were still around to buffer me from the cold, cruel world. I never took it personally when someone near and dear to me passed away, and it never crossed my mind that I would have to get old one day or that my body would eventually fail me. Any money that I earned back then was mine to use as I saw fit. I seldom had to share much of it with Uncle Sam. No pesky creditors waited in line with hands extended on payday. Not to mention the fact that, thanks to my youthful insouciance, I virtually slept straight through the Cuban Missile Crisis.

At the age of fifteen, I began working summers as a copyboy at the *Pittsburgh Press/Post-Gazette*. Pittsburgh had a morning and an evening paper at that time. These days, with the advent of the Internet and the proliferation of cable news, the city is struggling to keep one paper afloat. Every dollar I made while working summers at the paper I kept. In fact, I usually saved enough to pay for anything that I wanted throughout the school year.

Since I had no firsthand experience with a serious physical ailment, it never occurred to me that I might actually become ill. I considered myself immune from such things. Hospitals, therefore, represented a haven for those less fortunate, just some place where the sick went for help.

But the truth is that I wouldn't want to relive those days. I may have been lighthearted, but I was also shy, introverted, insecure, and, let's not mince words here, "out to lunch."

No, I'll gladly accept the hand that I'm dealt. Granted, seeing the world with such clarity has forced me to deal with certain life-and-death issues that I hadn't dealt with before, but I'm not complaining. Because all things considered, I know that it's a necessary progression. Among other things, maturity, which entails seeing the world in its true light, has its price, like everything else in this life—a troublesome side B to color the pleasant effects of side A.

Reaching middle age, living long enough to be able to see this somewhat offensive side B, is worth the aggravation. I'll grapple with death and old age if that's what it takes. In the big picture, I'll take a little diarrhea if it means ridding myself of the acne. Such is my newfound clarity. Such is my newfound midlife maturity.

Chapter 9: Wake Me When It's Over

IRONICALLY, ONE OF THE first things that hit me, having reached my mature, emotionally gifted, post-forty stage of life, was that my world had grown a bit stale. It didn't take long to notice that life, once known for its uncanny ability to keep me off balance, just wasn't keeping me pinned back on my heels like it used to. Life, the tricky old codger, just didn't have my number anymore. It appeared that much of my existence was becoming more familiar with each passing moment.

Suddenly, everything seemed passé. I could almost tell what people were going to say before they said it and could practically predict events before they happened. It was as if I had a knack for reading minds, even tell when someone was saying something rude about me. You know what they say about how your ears burn when you're being talked about? I could guess what his or her exact words might be, given the situation. I would say, "I bet I know exactly what this person said. He/she said 'that Robinson guy needs to shut up and mind his own ...'" Of course, I never heard the exact quote, so I never knew how accurate my assessment was. But I bet I've been pretty close to the remark on many occasions. You just develop a gut feeling for these things.

Imagine that. Midlife—the great eye-opener for me—had clued me in to the general predictability of it all, the reality that all good things get old with time. This situation makes for one interesting midlife irony. Call it the Peggy Lee Effect, named after the seductive songstress. Having gotten to a point in life when the world is an open book, one has to wonder, "Is that all there is?"

Don't get me wrong; this situation isn't hopeless. There are certain indicators that attest to the fact that I haven't seen it all. I have yet to receive definitive word on whether life exists on other planets, for starters, and I'm certainly no closer to finding out my ultimate fate, when and where I'll breathe my final breath. I take solace in the notion that such mysteries as Sasquatch and the Loch Ness Monster remain unsolved. I know I'll probably never figure some people out, and let's face it—I'm still learning certain pertinent facts about myself.

So, all things considered, I'm still picking it up as I go. But the damage is done. I've seen a lot in fifty-plus years. Experience has taught me well, perhaps a little *too* well. It seems to me that the bulk of this life and many of the situations that we encounter in our day-to-day affairs have a penchant for predictability. Once you've been around the block a few times, some of this stuff can get pretty old.

Having performed countless repetitions, encountered the same situations, and heard identical lines hundreds of times throughout a lifetime, some individuals might begin to feel as if they have seen just about all there was to be seen. Hence the phrase that is often echoed after an unusual occurrence: "Now I've seen everything!" Like the woman in the old Wendy's commercials, I sometimes ask myself, *Where's the beef?*

From my new, illuminated, middle-aged point of view, predicting certain aspects of human behavior and day-to-day events is getting to be a breeze. If you don't believe me, consider these real-life examples:

Example 1. When they were all living under my roof, I noticed that my children's behavior, once guaranteed to keep me guessing, had suddenly become telegraphed and unimaginative. It hurt to see just how easily I could see right through their little charades. I almost felt sorry for them—poor little devils. They had no idea what they were dealing with. After all, they were still on the same

Fighting the Effects of Gravity

level maturity-wise and I had crossed over to the other side and become a full-fledged guru in the game of life.

I suddenly found myself anticipating when they were about to hit me up for money or detecting when a power struggle was developing over the use of that evil device known as a telephone. Eventually, they all got cell phones, which quelled the skirmishes but created another annoyance, substituting old-fashioned ringing with annoying sirens, bells, wails, and rap tunes. I could even predict what the final outcome was going to be with a new boyfriend, based on his demeanor and behavior.

Example 2. Since reaching middle age, I find that I have this uncanny ability to give an immediate thumbs-up or -down to a first-run movie without the benefit of a private screening. I base my predictions solely on the endless previews that bombard the airwaves prior to release. I find myself watching the trailer for an upcoming feature and offering an immediate comment: "That looks good" or "Boy, I bet that's a loser!" I'll let you in on one secret. The tip-off for not-so-good cinematography seems to be when too much of the plot or all of the good jokes seem to be given away in the preview. Mark my words: if the trailer is a little too amusing, the movie probably isn't. I sometimes even have the confidence to give a movie a quick rating. "That looks like maybe three stars," I often wager.

While you might consider this capability a gift, an out-and-out case of clairvoyance, I know otherwise. I insist that I've seen so many motion pictures in my time that the similarities are becoming strikingly apparent. In other words, all movies are starting to look alike.

Example 3. After thirty-five years of marriage, my wife and I know each other's moves so well that we are even starting to think alike. Forget that notion of being on the same page. It's almost as if, to save time and effort, our brains have simply merged into one efficient unit.

Speech seems to be the biggest casualty of this merger. I'm hoping that our language skills won't, one day, become obsolete. I envision us awakening in the not-too-distant future to find ourselves finishing each other's sentences, like she and my mother are somehow able to do. Or worse, communicating through a simple series of hand motions, nods, and one-word rejoinders: "Yeah." "OK." "Right!"

Example 4. My parents, whom I once considered the poster couple for the unpredictable, have suddenly abdicated their throne. It's a sad sight to see so much of their behavior now a transparent shell. I wonder if they have actually been this predictable all along. The next time my mother gets wind of the fact that I'm not feeling well, I am willing to lay extremely heavy odds on her reaction. I know that she'll look at me in the same concerned way and ask me the same question that she's asked me since I was a baby: "What hurts you?" My father is almost certain to follow suit. "Son," he'll say with a strained look, "are you sick?"

Example 5. Politicians, meanwhile, are the most predictable of all species. If they are running in a tight race and fall behind in the polls, they're likely to say, "I don't believe in polls." If they are running ahead in these same polls, however, they'll take comfort in their lead and say something predictable, like "I've always said that my message was getting through to the voters. We're running a good race, and the American people have seen through the rhetoric of my opponent—yada, yada, yada." Translation: "I only believe in the polls when I'm winning."

Yes, life is getting to be a bit too easy to fathom these days, and it's got me thinking. Perhaps I'm being a bit melodramatic, but I sometimes worry that my existence will take on the appearance of the movie *Groundhog Day*.

Perhaps you recall this movie, in which a man played by Bill Murray is stuck in a virtual time warp, forced to relive the same day over and over, meeting the same people, awakening to the same annoying Sonny and Cher tune every single day, unable to return to his normal existence until he finally gets every detail of this day just right. Talk about your predictability nightmare. These circumstances aren't likely to befall me or anyone else anytime soon, but they're interesting to ponder nonetheless.

Fighting the Effects of Gravity

Motivated by the seeming sameness of it all, I see a surprising number of my middle-aged brethren pushing the limits of rational thinking in a desperate attempt to sever the monotony. I have witnessed members of my age group, as well as a healthy contingent of adventurous pre-midlifers, performing stunts that defy gravity, not to mention good sense.

I have personally observed these weekend daredevils: bungee-jumping from cranes; going whitewater rafting in rapids that were obviously better off left unrafted; dangling from mountains that rise up at a ninety-degree angle from the earth and should, therefore, never be dangled from; hang-gliding from mountains; and skydiving from airplanes.

Then, of course, you get the inevitable variations: bungee-jumping from bridges; parachuting from bridges; two leapers jumping "tandem" (attached at the chest by small hooks, holding on to each other for dear life) while parachuting from a bridge; parachuting from mountains; climbing up the side of a building utilizing suction cups on the knees and hands; and parachuting from a fifty-story building. I have yet to see anyone bungee jump from a moving airplane, but the night is still young.

These activities give a whole new meaning to the term "weekend warrior." Whatever happened to the simple pursuits, such as flag football and horseback riding? Even the modern-day paintball competitions—infantile and warlike as they may be—strike a happy medium. Combatants can wear protective headgear and other padding, shoot realistic weapons, and pretend that they're putting their lives and the lives of friends and relatives in peril.

I can only imagine what might happen to me if I attempted any of these acts of daring. I've incurred significant bodily harm while engaging in activities considerably less dangerous than the above. When I was twenty-six, I sprained my ankle so badly during an extremely low-impact game of touch football at a family picnic that I had to be carried to my car by my brother-in-law.

While horsing around with a friend at the age of ten, I tore ligaments in my right ankle when I momentarily lost sight of my athletic shortcomings and leaped off a daunting flight of four or five steps that joined our front walk to our front porch and landed awkwardly on my right foot. No, I didn't take a shot of a painkiller like my father and return to playtime—no crowd, no glory—but my leg was in a cast up to the knee for six weeks.

My father, James Sr., as I have documented earlier, is the famous athlete of the family. But he often tells a story of how he broke his nose when, in a serious lapse of judgment and youthful insouciance (I'm being kind; he was stupid), he jumped off his roof. He fashioned an umbrella into a makeshift cape, trying to imitate Superman. Give him an A for creativity, at least. (I don't want to get into the sheer lunacy of such an attempt except to say that at least I was only foolhardy enough to attempt the front steps.)

Fortunately, he was a mere twelve-year-old adventure seeker at the time. A similar leap attempted as a middle-ager would surely have resulted in his being fitted for a full-body cast.

My sad stories aside, I would wager that if you ask these daredevils why they have chosen to undertake such risky business, they would have a blanket statement prepared: "Oh, just for the sheer challenge of it."

But don't let them fool you, these tricksters. They're merely covering their tracks. If they were honest, these risk-takers would come clean. They would admit that they are simply bored as the dickens and that the real reason they risk life and limb is not for nobility's sake but for a cheap thrill, to get the blood going—in the vernacular, to "get a rush."

Quite an interesting notion, this "rush." While I see nothing wrong with someone wanting to put a little zing into his or her life, this rush notion has me a little concerned. I get as mentally wearied as the next person, but I would have to stop short of cheating death just to get the old adrenaline pumping. I'll just have to be satisfied with whatever charge I can muster from watching the latest Sly Stallone action flick. Not that I have much choice in the matter.

Heights, I would have to say, are not my strong suit. I get shaky when I advance any higher than the third rung of a five-rung stepladder while changing a light bulb. I find myself holding on to the top step of the ladder for support with one hand and tentatively changing the light bulb with the other. If I were to leap from a twenty-story building with only a few seconds to open a parachute, I would fear a sudden "rush" that would see me rushing to the nearest bathroom to rescue my undergarments.

I don't want to rain on anyone's parade, but the law of diminishing returns also looms large in this scenario. It seems that if one needs, at this juncture, to leap from a three-thousand-foot precipice with only a piece of glorified spandex stretching between him and his maker to escape boredom, what would he do for an encore?

I foresee sizable problems on the horizon. I sense that, as these individuals advance in age, they will become all the more willing to risk their necks for the almighty rush. In a last-ditch, all-out effort to escape the clutches of the infamous Peggy Lee Effect, no mountain will be considered too high, no river too wide, no bungee cord too thin.

This might not be at the top of anyone's list of concerns, but I have to wonder: where will it end, people? The bar will, in effect, have been raised forever. When the dust settles, all previous notions of what is and what isn't considered foolhardy will have been erased from our minds. I'm sure you're familiar with the human penchant for one-upsmanship. We like nothing better than to top one another. The *Guinness World Records* is full of regular folks turned record holders who couldn't leave well enough alone. What seems amazing today will surely be a real yawner tomorrow.

The late Evel Knievel's ill-fated, albeit ambitious, attempt to traverse Snake River Canyon in the early 1970s utilizing a steam-thrust "skycycle" was overshadowed not long after by his son Robbie, who cleared a more realistic 228-foot section of the Grand Canyon on a conventional 500cc motorcycle. Had son Robbie failed, he would have plunged 2,500 feet to the canyon floor. Evel, who was never able to get permission to do the Grand Canyon jump, once soared over fourteen Greyhound buses—a record distance of 190 feet. Robbie leapfrogged his father's record when he soared like the proverbial eagle over thirty limousines.

The late, great master Harry Houdini was famous for his escape tricks, but he also made a ten-thousand-pound elephant disappear in 1918. Magician David Copperfield, however, upped Harry's ante by making the Statue of Liberty, a seven-ton Lear jet, and the Orient Express luxury train vanish before a live TV audience. For an encore, he levitated across the same Grand Canyon that the Knievel clan found so alluring. I'm not exactly sure what drives illusionist, magician, and "endurance artist" David Blaine. Some people, including the pundits at the *New York Times*, have labeled him a modern-day Houdini. He strikes me as a bit off the wall.

The high-wire feats of Karl Wallenda, who fell to his death in 1978 while walking on a wire between two hotels 120 feet above the ground in Puerto Rico, meanwhile already seems pretty tame.

Last summer, I watched a daring but totally unheralded performer walk a tightrope that stretched over a 100-or-so-foot-section of a local amusement park that looked to be at least 150 feet from the ground. He had nothing to break his fall other than the Raging Rapids, and he probably received little more for his trouble than one of those doughy fried funnel cakes with the powdered sugar on top—the real reason we go to the park. Despite the obvious danger, I must admit that I calmly continued to gawk at the scenery and suck down my French fries during his journey.

But I think it's time we called a truce. I see no need to continue such hijinks. To you extreme thrill seekers I have only one thing to say: "Get a life." Yeah, you heard me, get a life. You midlife adrenaline junkies are merely getting a temporary high, trying to stave off that final pass through the checker flag. Why risk your life? The way they're making roller coasters nowadays, why bother with the crazy stuff? Drink a cranked-up cup of Starbucks coffee every morning like everyone else. Try one of those high-energy drinks—they'll keep you wired. One can of 5-Hour Energy would have me speaking in tongues. Just don't go putting that white powdery stuff up your nose.

As my mother used to say to me, "Just settle down!" Stop the madness. Step away from the bungee cords, go easy on the hard-core whitewater rafting, and climb a mountain that doesn't require you to dangle your full bodyweight from a tiny rock. We midlifers don't need to walk on the wild side; we need to prepare ourselves for the tests that are about to come. Save the crazy stuff for the professionals. They have enough loose bolts for all of us. Your legacy speaks for itself, Evel Knievel. David Blaine, I'm still trying to figure you out. You're the man for this century, David Copperfield. Rest in peace, Harry Houdini, you magnificent bastard. Save your energy, middle-aged crazies. Your bucket list is calling.

Chapter 10: Or Is It Chapter 9? I Forget.

Putting a Face on the Brain Cramp

HAVING STUMBLED INTO THIS not-so-brave new world known as midlife, I find that my brain isn't functioning quite the way it used to. You wouldn't know it to look at me, but my mental capacities are, at times, gasping for breath. Though, as I've already discussed, I can see the workings of society a lot more clearly than I could in my pre-midlife days, I'm just not thinking with the same clarity as I did before. Oh, I can still speak in coherent sentences and walk and chew gum at the same time. I can add and subtract and even perform some fairly complex mathematical functions in my head without the use of a calculator. I actually still do consider myself a fairly intelligent being. But there are breakdowns, times when simple thought processing goes awry. Memory lapses, the so-called brain cramp, have become an all-too-common affair, a way of life if you will, and I can't say as I like it.

Oftentimes, my brain feels more like an aging computer. While there still may be plenty of room on the hard drive, my RAM—the running memory that keeps the computer going smoothly from one program to another—seems insufficient. It clicks and sputters, and that "program not responding" message keeps coming up. Control, alt, delete is not an option. It appears that I had a lot more RAM when I was younger.

To be specific, why is it that I find myself standing in front of an open refrigerator like a flesh-eating zombie, wondering why I came into the kitchen in the first place? While this type of event happened when I was younger—eight years old or so—it had nothing to do with memory loss. I was just being a pain in the butt. I was hungry, or bored, and couldn't find anything I wanted to eat. "There's nothing to eat," I eventually ended up whining to my mother.

At that age, generous portions of roast duck, fried chicken, and crème brulée could have jumped out at me and sung a Stephen Foster medley and I still would have whined and cried.

Eventually I got the desired response from my ever-patient mother: "Son, what do you want?"

But in my middle years, it's more a matter of the insidious brain cramp, also known as a memory lapse or blank spot, an apparent brain malfunction that surfaces at middle age. In this condition, the brain cramps and stutters like a car that won't start. I eventually realize—once my mind has cleared—that I'm staring down a jar of Hellman's Mayonnaise for no reason and that my original mission was not to look for food but to search for my slippers or take my medication, which also happens to located in the kitchen. Somehow I just got distracted along the way. But not to worry, I'm used to it by now. I may get a little disgusted, sigh, and grimace, but it's all part of the new way of things.

The middle-aged brain must be full of these infamous blank spots. If you took a close look at the landscape of the brain I'm sure you would see blocks of fertile ground inundated with small areas of wasteland that can no longer sustain life. Names appear to be one of the main culprits. I have noticed that we have developed this annoying way of covering up for our lack of name recognition by saying, "You know, what's-his-name ..." or, worse yet, "what's-her-face." These terms have become a part of the midlife speech pattern. Webster hasn't quite caught the hint yet, but there's still time: "What's-her-face—a term used, often by a middle-aged

Fighting the Effects of Gravity

adult, when he or she can't think of a proper name or title. See lapse." We know when a blank spot is coming, so we just plug them in to keep things rolling smoothly.

My wife is famous for it. She will try to relay a story to me told to her by one of our daughters, and it sounds something like this: "Erin told me that Jaime told her that what's-his-name was really mad because Bill never got home last night and that what's-her-face knew about it but didn't tell her. She makes me sick."

"You're probably right," I say in lieu of "I didn't understand a word you just said." It's best just to go along with it.

Then there's the quick version: "Did you talk to "what's-her-face" today?" I usually wait for some sort of confirmation on that one. "You know, Bill." Then I speak.

Often, when trying to come up with a name, a short-term memory lapse leads to an episode of partial recall. I'll think hard for a few minutes and eventually come up with the first name in question, but the last name still evades me, or vice versa. It's as if my brain is feeding me the information in pieces just to tick me off.

The condition even appears to be contagious. Sometimes I'll struggle to remember a name and I'll bring another person my age into the fray and both of us will go blank. On rare occasions, we'll draw a trifecta—a perfect storm of a three stammering midlifers who can't remember one simple piece of information. It's the damndest thing. We'll stand there and look at each other, gesturing frantically with our hands searching for the designation, all the while saying, "Oh yeah, I know who you mean." Sometimes one of us might say, "Now, that's going to drive me crazy all day until I remember it." We finally give up, laugh it off, and chalk it up to Alzheimer's disease. Then later that same day or perhaps even the next day, the name will come to me, only to be gone again a few hours later. My guess is the same thing is happening to the other two middle-aged stooges. I can see them both walking around all day and then suddenly proclaiming, "Oh yeah, that was it." Ideally, we should all meet up again and compare notes. Then the mysterious name quietly slips into the archives again.

It's as if the middle-aged brain is playing a mean-spirited game of peek-a-boo.

In one instance, I forgot the name of my cable company—I had only made monthly checks payable to this company for ten years or so—and was forced to look it up in the Yellow Pages. The white pages were useless because I would need the name of the company to find it. You know what I mean. Well, an instant before I came to the cable company listings, the name of this cable giant mysteriously popped into my head. Come on, now, that's not funny!

Sometimes the mind can be particularly cruel. A piece of information may not just be a little evasive—one of those "it's on the tip of my tongue" things—but may seemingly be wiped from the memory banks altogether so that it has to be relearned. I sometimes wrack my brain to come up with some name or term, and when I finally manage to figure it out it seems almost foreign. I'll find myself saying, "Wow, I would have never come up with that one."

Something tells me that this situation is only going to get worse. I can't help but notice that my mother can't attach any of her grandchildren to the right name the first time out anymore. When she greets one of them, she sometimes can't immediately ascertain which of my three offspring she is addressing and ends up rattling off all three of their names like it's some kind of confused roll call: "Hi, uh, Jaime, uh, Erin, uh, Kim." Maybe it would help if they wore name tags. And to make matters worse, these children have married and begun to have offspring of their own. I'm an only child, so she was spared the embarrassment on that level.

I recall my grandmother, my mother's mother, however, having the same lapses with my mother and her five sisters and brothers, except there were six of them and therefore more room for error. As my grandmother got older, the thirteen grandchildren got tossed into the inventory with the six children: "Vonda, uh, Edgar, uh, Kathy, uh, Buddy …" Toward the end of her life, the great-grandchildren could get thrown into the mix too.

Fighting the Effects of Gravity

Despite these lapses, however, my grandmother—Grammy, as we called her—remained mentally sharp until the day she died. We all grew to love those blank spots because they belonged to her.

Then there is the issue of long-term vs. short-term memory. It concerns me that, while I can remember names and events from the Nixon-Kennedy days, items from the Bush-Cheney era are fading fast. Obama-What's-His-Name is too close to call. I remember that Dick Cheney shot one of his buddies on a hunting trip. Poor guy. What was the unlucky shootee's name? Ronald Reagan's vice-president was, uh? Oh well.

My father, a retired Presbyterian minister, received his first calling to the ministry in 1959 to a church in Wichita, Kansas. My mother, my father, and I all look back with mutual distain upon this time in life for a number of reasons.

Consider that we were forced to leave our home in Pittsburgh, Pennsylvania, where we had lived for most of our lives and where the majority of our immediate family resided. I took it particularly hard. I think I cried all the way to Virginia. We were headed to the Wichita area not because it was a hotbed of economic growth but because it was the only city where my father received a job offer after graduating from seminary. The newly ordained Rev. Robinson made $4,500 a year for his first pastoral position. While you might think that, considering inflation, this salary was sufficient back then, think again. We laugh about how my father often sat on the porch waiting for the mailman—Henry, a name that will live in infamy—to bring his check.

Also, consider that the good reverend walked into a transitional situation at the church—Brotherhood Church as it happened to be called—and upon his arrival, half of the congregation, two hundred members, went elsewhere.

Despite these issues, this time in life seems to be, for some odd reason, particularly fertile ground for me in terms of recalling names and other impertinent details. My father also has great recall of these days, and we talk about them often.

"Remember so-and-so," I ask my father, pulling the name of a particular sixteen-year-old boy from his youth group out of the air.

"Oh yeah," he says, amazed at my recall. "He was a terrible kid. I wanted to choke him. How do you remember that?"

"And how about that man with the thick glasses? I asked once. "He could barely see the hymn book, but he had that great singing voice."

"No," he said with a quizzical look on his face, "I don't remember him."

My father was asked to direct a Presbyterian summer camp in Ponca City, Oklahoma, during the summer of 1960. Amazingly, I can give you a play-by-play of the happenings, lame as they may have been.

We often reminisce about the campers, the counselors, and the menacing-looking tarantulas that ran amok throughout the campgrounds. I also remember the irritating Presbyterian camp songs we sang at night by the campfire—"We are the Presbyterian Kids," to name one. I mean, really, how corny can you get?

"You pulled your hamstring chasing one of those annoying campers didn't you?" I ask. "I remember you hobbling around." I've stumped him again.

"Man," he says, "you remember everything!"

For God's sake, that was half a century ago. I was a Cub Scout. Ask me what I had for dinner last night. Go ahead, ask me. I'm thinking. Should my brain be behaving like this? Is this thought processing normal?

And what's all the talk about brain cells? I keep hearing that I am losing brain cells. Where are they going? I need specifics. How many brain cells did I start with, and how many do I have now? I have seen one-hundred-year-old people with alert minds. They should only have a few brain cells left by this time. I'm not feeling this one.

But through it all there is this constant fear of a serious mental issue. As much as we joke around about how we're getting Alzheimer's when a mental breakdown occurs, I suspect that many of us actually do worry as much about dementia as much as we do about cancer and other deadly diseases.

A few years back, I heard an MD on a morning TV show draw the following distinction between the normal forgetfulness that comes with aging and full-blown dementia: "If you forget your wife's name," he said, "it's not a big deal. If you forget you have a wife, that's definitely a big deal."

Matt Lauer got a real kick out of it. I, on the other hand, have used it as a point of reference every time my middle-aged brain has left me in the lurch—wondering just how far gone I really am. I have even put my own little spin on the exercise. I figure, if I forget where I put my keys, no sweat, if I find my keys in the refrigerator—uh-oh.

So the next time you're standing like a zombie in front of a wide-open refrigerator, check for your keys. If they're not there, grab the mayo, count your lucky stars, and take your medication— that's probably why you came into the kitchen in the first place.

Now I remember, Ronald Reagan's vice president—George Bush! But which one?

Chapter 11: Beware the Middle-Age Dance

Will you, won't you, will you, won't you, will you join the dance?
Lewis Carroll

HAVE YOU EVER DONE anything you didn't want to do? Taken one for the team? Perhaps your mother made you take piano or forced you to suffer through dance lessons as a kid. I hear that there are of lot of accomplished artists such as Billy Joel and Marvin Hamlisch who wouldn't be stars if their mothers hadn't strong-armed them to stay cooped up inside the house and practice scales. Imagine the world without "Piano Man" and "The Way We Were." Well, I certainly hope for their sake that they feel it was worth the trouble. But for every Billy and Marvin there is a middle-aged adult who is still miffed at his mother for making him sit at the piano and take lessons while his friends were outside playing football.

While it would be wise to pay your taxes, obey traffic signs, and avoid recreational drug use, the time has come to show your true mettle. As mentally aroused candidates for senior citizenship, it's time for all of us to stand up and make our voices heard, make up for all the times that we walked off silently into the night. That's why, having reached my middle years in one piece, I have to make it clear right here and now—this dance thing, I just don't get it.

As a middle-ager, I have often sat at parties, weddings, and other social functions and watched as others danced. I would track them as they'd come and go, doing their own thing, the one dance that makes them who they are, as pitiful as it may be. I admit it, there are times when I chuckled at some of the moves—okay, laughed out loud if I must admit it. But what goes around tends to come back toward the instigator with a vengeance. My lack of participation seldom goes unnoticed. My observations are always interrupted by those bullies who seek to coerce me into giving my own rendition. Invariably, I catch the well-trained eye of the dance police. "Don't you dance?" they ask. Busted!

I have personally observed tentative, nondancing individuals being accosted and yanked onto the dance floor by overzealous funsters. What's the theory behind this behavior? It's tantamount to throwing a nonswimmer into ten feet of water. Why put someone in a position where he or she is going to have to thrash about? When it comes to shaking one's tail feather, common wisdom somehow dictates that it has to be all or nothing. Everyone has fun or no one does.

I can recall adult dance chaperones—usually parents of my classmates and friends—exhorting me to dance, informing me when I walked in the door at the tender age of twelve that, in fact, they "couldn't wait to see me dance." I'm not sure why they felt the need to put the spotlight on me in this manner. Perhaps I just didn't look the part. I'm not surprised, though. I'm the type of person who never quite looks the part when it some to just about any of life's pursuits, no matter how mundane. I can't tell you how many times I've heard someone say incredulously, "I just can't imagine you doing that."

Well, at any rate, I couldn't perform under that kind of pressure. No, I wasn't made that way. Shy and self-conscious individual that I was, I simply laid low until the coast was clear. I kept quiet and blended in with the woodwork. Yeah, that's right—I caved. Just hearing such an intimidating statement was enough to keep

Fighting the Effects of Gravity

me glued to a chair for the remainder of the proceedings. The thought of all eyes being trained on me while I boogied down and shook my so-called moneymaker to music was simply too much to bear.

As fate would have it, however, I would go on to cut a mean rug in later years. I danced in high school, but only after one of my more "worldly" friends had showed me the latest steps in private. One worldly friend in particular ushered me to the boy's room and quickly took me through some of the new dance moves.

Even then, the moves didn't come easily, but I practiced them on my own until I felt confident enough to display them for my peers. Thinking back, this procedure seems like an awful lot of work. I was never terribly comfortable at it. But I went through this ordeal because the last thing that I wanted was to be labeled a teenage wallflower. But things have changed. I don't really mind being called a wallflower at this stage. I'm not looking for validation or acceptance. I don't want a date for the prom. I just want to get some things in order before the final bell rings. Being considered a decorative part of a barricade suits me just fine. I'm cranky. I'm still a little sore over some of the things that have transpired over my lifetime. I'm pushing sixty, and frankly, I don't care.

Remember *American Bandstand*—Dick Clark standing at his podium as teenagers danced the latest dances to the latest music? Remember the monkey and the twist and the mashed potato? Who could forget the segment of the show where contestants were asked to rate new records? "I like the beat and the lyrics," the youth would say, "I give it a six."

But, like a fad, dances seem to come and go. As we progress in age, we no longer have the time or the desire to learn every new dance craze. Adulthood takes us into other directions and we begin to lose touch. By the time we reach middle age, we are spectators to the whole affair. For some of us, Arthur Murray takes over. We learn grown-up, sophisticated dances like the cha-cha and the fox trot and the merengue, dances that stand the test of time.

But A. Murray just isn't all that fly. He can't plug us into the latest steps. That's when things get interesting. That's when some people of the midlife persuasion and beyond attempt an all-out assault on past glory.

From my vantage point, a unique process occurs during midlife that causes illusions of grandeur in the middle-aged and makes them think that they can dance like teenagers. It's as if some mysterious biological clock kicks in and tells them that learning the latest dance steps is essential if they are to die with dignity. It's difficult to say what triggers this event. Perhaps it's the cumulative effect of years of watching Dick Clark and Co. and *Soul Train*. At any rate, a rite of passage occurs in which the misguided midlifers make a feeble attempt to reclaim their dance prowess by way of the naïve, unsuspecting younger generation.

The following scene is played out daily in thousands of family get-togethers across the country. Perhaps you have witnessed the drama at one time or another.

Picture this: A family gathering. Several middle-aged opportunists mill around, laughing and eating. They look innocent enough, but don't be fooled. They are about to undergo a startling transformation. With no warning, the sound of music fills the air. The well-behaved opportunists suddenly become wild with dance fever. The transformation has begun.

My mother, who claims to have been quite a dancer in her time, was always at the center of this controversy. I always dubbed her "the ringleader" when it came to this dancing frenzy. "Your father never danced," she has always said—I guess he never took the time to wander off into the men's room and solicit dance steps from his college buddies. "I was always out on the dance floor dancing with my guy friends." I don't ever recall her saying what boogying she did—the jitterbug would be my guess.

When the music started to play at these functions, something came over her. I guess she figured that if she could do the dances from her day, she should be able to pick up the modern movements just as easily, but it never quite worked out that way. She would seize the moment and ask one of the "with it" teens or preteens in the family to help her get her middle-aged groove on. "Come on, Albie," she would say to her nephew. "Show us how to do it."

My cousin Albie, the chosen one, would dutifully comply and make the dance look so easy that it gave my mother—and any other oldsters who also wanted to learn—a false sense of security. Albie, oddly enough, now fifty-four, dances like my uncle Earl did in his younger days. Earl, my mother's younger brother at seventy-eight, now shies away from the dance floor altogether. Apparently, a baton has been passed between the two at some point, although I'm not sure if either one of them knows it. Albie displays the unattractive dancer's overbite and moves like every part of his body hurts. I still watch. Oh how the pendulum swings.

Believing that they could learn this dance instantly, the opportunists would jump in without hesitation. That's when things got interesting. The resulting movements bore little or no resemblance to those that had just been displayed. As a matter of fact, they seldom bore any resemblance to any dance I had ever seen.

Refusing to obey orders, their bodies betrayed them. Arms and legs became instruments of destruction, thrashing about with no apparent motive or sense of order. The scene looked like a preview from some gang-oriented flick where two very diverse elements clash, a la the Jets and Sharks from *West Side Story*. Frankenstein meets the Rockettes comes immediately to mind.

Perhaps I was the smart one of the group. I knew better than to think that I could learn a dance on sight. My high school dance-instructor friend was nowhere to be found, and I hugged the sideline like a veteran wide receiver. My mother and the other possessed, middle-aged family members eventually became frustrated and broke into dances that they could do, namely the twist, the swim, the jerk, the frug, the Charleston, and, when all else failed, the hokey-pokey.

Seeing how ridiculous they looked, these nondancers were able to laugh at themselves. In so doing, the spell was broken. Once again, they realized the error of their ways. They walked away knowing that they had a better chance of walking on water than doing the dances that they had just seen performed. My mother would often end the ritual with the remark "You make it look so easy!"

There is a very good reason why we older folk are doomed to fail when it comes to learning nonchoreographed movement. Unbeknownst to us, we undergo certain physical changes between the time when we dance by osmosis and the time when we reach middle age. Some would seek to blame our problems on "rhythm," casually branding some poor souls with the tag of "totally rhythmless."

How cruel. I consider this remark both inaccurate and offensive, especially when it's directed at me. I would wager that there is no statute of limitations on rhythm and, excluding a few glaring exceptions, everyone is endowed with it. Whether it's at age fifty or fifteen, rhythm, like the earth and the stars, is a constant. No, in all likelihood, rhythm is not the culprit. It's our coordination that's shot all to the devil's dungeon. Let me explain.

The middle-aged brain, which in its younger days was capable of visualizing an event such as dance and sending out clear-cut instructions to all parties involved, now appears to be suspect. In its advanced stages, it appears incapable of coordinating all of the movements necessary to pull off an intricate maneuver. It doesn't seem to have the wherewithal to execute an all-out effort where arms, legs, and feet move in concert. Although all of the principles may be willing, something is lost in the translation. The results must sound similar to the Abbott and Costello "Who's on First?" skit.

Just imagine the confusion:

Brain: Okay, everybody, listen up! Right leg first.
Right leg: Right leg first what?
Brain: Now left leg.
Left leg: Huh?

Fighting the Effects of Gravity

Brain: No, left arm up, right leg left.
Left arm: Huh?
Feet: Shouldn't we be doing something?
Brain: Left arm, right foot, left leg. Now hear this, all extremities: you're on your own!

Midlife dancing is a totally different kind of dancing altogether. It's old-people dancing, free-style dancing, I-don't-know-what-the-heck-I'm-doing-but-I'll-give-it-a-shot dancing. If you watch older people dance, you'll see that it doesn't take knowing any particular type of dance as much as it takes total inhibition—a good strong Captain and Coke certainly wouldn't hurt the cause—and some level of coordination. Simply put, they wing it. Some display a high level of coordination; others, well, stick to the basics.

Sure, there are times when, having watched one couple after another display their skills—and I use that term loosely—I join the fray. But I do it now not because I feel pressured but because I just don't care. I guess I'm becoming more like my father. I see the dances that he does with his great-grandchildren, and it's pretty obvious that he is in the "oh, screw it" stage. Friends and other relatives threaten to display his moves on Facebook. I'm getting there, but I'm definitely not in that neighborhood yet.

Debbie is always quick to tell everyone at a function who asks that "we don't dance." She, in effect, has declared us off limits—the dance version of the demilitarized zone—essentially labeled us as dance voyeurs. She has wrapped some of that yellow police tape around our table. But why should we have to explain this? Did tribal warriors in Africa ever strong-arm the more timid among them into doing ceremonial dances so that fun could be had by all? Somehow, I doubt it.

Let me put it to you straight: if you want to dance, then dance. If you don't, then don't. Don't let some pushy half-wit muscle you onto the dance floor of life and make you do something you don't want to do. Don't let your mother force you to play piano. You're at a wedding reception, not a prom. A bride is fixin' to throw a bouquet. The groom is gonna toss a garter to a bunch of dudes wearing rented tuxedos. You're half-a-hundred, for God's sake. Mortality is calling. Put your foot down. And don't look back.

Chapter 12: I Don't Want to Get Old, and You Can't Make Me!

Man fools himself. He prays for long life, and he fears old age.
Chinese proverb

    Not surprisingly, it wasn't too long after I had reached the middle portion of my being that yet another of life's bigger pictures came sharply into focus. After a lifetime of not fully comprehending the true progression of things, life's basic blueprint suddenly burst into my consciousness. There it was in black and white. I was immediately stunned by the clarity of the message. In an instant, I knew exactly where I stood.
    It was almost as if I were staring at one of those maps that they place at strategic points in shopping malls to help confused shoppers, only mine looked something like this:

YOUTH	MIDDLE AGE	OLD AGE	DEATH**
	⇧		
	You are here		

** *Tentatively scheduled; could occur at any time.*

The order of things was suddenly crystal clear. I took this visual enlightenment to mean the following: I was young once, now I'm in life's mid-section, old age is next on the horizon (if this scenario plays out), and death will occur sooner or later, preferably later, say, after eighty years or so of living.

Having beheld this all-encompassing vision, my main goal in life has changed dramatically. Old age is no longer just a meaningless title; it's where I'll eventually end up (if I live long enough). My priorities, therefore, are totally askew. Having settled into my middle years, my focus should not center around making money and acquiring glitzy goods but around survival. My best shot, it seems, and my overall goal at this stage should be to get old, to put the moves on the grim reaper long enough to reach old age. Simply put, I have but two choices: I can either get old or I can die trying.

But now that the secret is out, I must admit that I'm not at all happy with this startling mandate. First of all, I have a problem with the inevitability aspect, the like-it-or-lump-it tone that seems to permeate the whole message. I consider it to be a highly insensitive ultimatum. I have to wonder, at what point did I lose control? Have I no choice in the matter?

The obvious lack of input reminds me of the days when I was a five-year-old and my mother neatly laid out the clothes on my bed that I was to wear that day. It seems apparent that life has carefully chosen my wardrobe for the duration of my being, and it doesn't seem quite fair.

But more importantly, I see a much bigger problem with this declaration. I detect a major fly in the ointment, a Catch-22 that needs to be addressed before we go any further. As a newly enlightened midlifer, staring into the face of old age, I feel that the time has come to ask the difficult questions.

My major concern is as follows: if reaching senior-citizen status is considered to be my one true goal, the place I should aspire to reach, why is it that I don't want to get old? It seems odd that, even though old age is the one and only game in town, all I want to do is take my ball and go home. Don't get me wrong. I

Fighting the Effects of Gravity

want to live. It's just that I'm not terribly thrilled with the prospect of getting old! There's something amiss here, people. Isn't this what they now consider an oxymoron? Am I supposed to be delightfully if not insanely happy about getting old or what?

To make matters worse, I haven't come totally clean. To be honest with you, I'm not looking forward to this little promotion in the least. At my age, if I'm going to get all psyched up for something, I find such events as vacations at the shore, Christmas, payday, Kenny G concerts, and the possibility of meaningful sexual contact to be much more enticing. If I have to, I'll add growing old to my list. But I assure you, my heart won't be in it. As my daughter would say in twenty-first-century homeboy slang, "I don't have that to do."

I must admit that I sometimes fantasize about circumventing old age altogether. Yeah, between you and me, if I knew there was some kind of an elderly detour—a viable way to bypass part three of the aging process—I would definitely give it some consideration. Just show me the detour signs, and I'll find my own way when the time comes. I know, you think I'm losing my mind, that there's no place else to go but old age. But before you brand me a lunatic, let's think about it for a moment.

Take a look at a few of these rather unique alternatives:

Alternative #1: What about a fountain of youth? I've never considered the possibility in the past, but faced with the prospect of old age, I find myself contemplating the existence of such a fountain. I wonder where it would it be located. What would it look like? Would it take on the appearance of a true fountain similar to the ones found in parks, the ones that feature water spewing from a statue's mouth? Something artsy in nature? Or would it approximate a common watering hole, but with panache, a drinking fountain with a kick?

While we're on the subject, what exactly would one do with such a fountain? Does one actually ingest the water, drink it like a potion to reap the benefits, swim in it, or simply become younger by association, just kind of watching the years slip away as you admire the view? And if we did partake of the liquid, would a single drink do the trick or would the effects wear off, necessitating annual pilgrimages for booster gulps?

The movie *Death Becomes Her* centered around a magic potion that provided endless life. Unfortunately, this movie also pointed out the foibles of this notion, the fact that human body parts aren't meant to last forever.

But this is fantasy. I have to wonder: if such a youth-oriented geyser exists (in whatever form), why have I heard no mention of it? Why haven't I seen a pictorial layout in *Life* magazine or watched tearful testimonials from youthful transformees on some TV newsmagazine?

Wouldn't this fount be a celebrity magnet? The tabloids would have a field day. Wouldn't youth seekers of all ages flock to this drinking mecca like there's no tomorrow? (Which there may not be.) I would expect long lines stretching halfway around the continent. Wouldn't it make a serious dent in the plastic-surgery business? With this society's fascination with drinking bottled water, why hasn't someone by now at least acted as if they managed to bottle a youthful elixir?

No, something tells me I'm fishing in the wrong lake here, that any effects from such a fountain would be more mental than physical. If there is a fountain of youth it can best be found in a Beverly Hills plastic surgeon's office.

Alternative #2: I have to admit that, as of late, the life of a vampire has piqued my interest a bit. Granted, I've never actually seen one in the flesh, but allow me to cite a number of valid reasons for my newfound curiosity: First of all, I am impressed by the vampire's ability to change into a winged mammal at the drop of a hat. It strikes me as an extremely efficient mode of transportation.

Second, from what I've observed, vampires don't show their age despite the fact that they are often purported to be hundreds of years old. And, third, I am well aware of their problem with sunlight. (They spontaneously combust, in case you didn't know.)

Fighting the Effects of Gravity

However, what with the depletion of the ozone, I figure it makes good sense to avoid the sun's rays anyway. Maybe a strong sun block would do the trick.

Of course, I'm no stranger to the downside. That stake-in-the-heart thing sounds a bit uncomfortable, spending my nights in a coffin has certain claustrophobic undertones, and what with the AIDS epidemic in full swing, I don't cotton much to a vampire's free-wheeling, bite-the-neck-of-anything-that-moves lifestyle. I certainly wouldn't want to risk drawing blood from a drug or alcohol abuser. The constant exchange of bodily fluids is just asking for trouble.

But let's not give up hope. Given today's technology, perhaps some sort of synthetic plasma could be developed. Or maybe these alleged siphoners of blood could be offered plasma gum to chew or patches to wear to take the edge off. Otherwise, I think that I'm a little too meticulous for this one.

Alternative #3: There was a time when I entertained the notion of—don't be offended; it's just a thought—auctioning my soul to the Devil. While you may gasp, striking a deal with the Dark One might not be such a bad idea after all. Yes, the transaction sounds ominous, but just maybe the shortcomings are a tad overrated. Granted, I would be a bit concerned about what my role would be once the deal was done, but I'm willing to give it some thought. I figure, what's the worst that the Evil One can do to me? Life hasn't exactly been a romp in the park for me up to this point. Yeah, who knows, maybe I've taken some of his best shots already. Perhaps His Darkness and I could work something out, credit for time served, perhaps. Considering the way I've behaved during the past forty-five years, who's to say that I'm not already under contract? Can I get an amen? I mean ... whatever.

Okay, okay, so I'm reaching. Perhaps I've been watching too many movies. I won't be drinking from any fountain of youth anytime soon, there is no such thing as a vampire, and I'm not about to put my soul on the auction block. But, hey, I'm struggling. As my kids would tell me, "Dad, you're trippin'." The obvious fact is that we have a problem here. The idea that I'm even contemplating such far-out alternatives tells you where my head is.

The fact remains that, at a time when I should be looking upon old age as a savior, my one and only option, I'm looking for a way out. Instead of awaiting what lies in store for me in my next stage of life, I'm digging in my heels. You would think that my mother was standing in front of me, spoon in hand, trying to coax me into swallowing a heaping tablespoon of cough syrup or handing me four or five of those dreadful baby aspirin tablets to chew.

Ingesting baby aspirin tablets is an experience that sticks in your mind. Even as an adult, my wife compares the taste of certain unappealing snack foods to baby aspirin. Looking back, I think I would have rather had the fever. Once you taste one of these orange-flavored treats, you never really forget the sensation.

But it's not just me. I have a sneaking suspicion that I have a lot of silent support from my fellow middle-agers out there. I know for certain that none of us is all that anxious to get old. I don't ever recall hearing any resounding pro-old-age sentiment, such as "I can't wait to get old!" or "You're nothing if you're not seventy!" And it seems unlikely that I ever will.

Having had some time to ponder this dilemma, I think I may have stumbled upon the central issue. I have come to the conclusion that we're just not very comfortable with the notion of getting old, and there's a good reason why. Old age has a serious PR problem. When it comes to the subject of growing old, in fact, we think the worst. Since there's no stopping the aging process, it's up to us to do what's necessary to alter our perception.

For instance, as it stands now, I can't help but view reaching the final phase of life to be a hollow victory, a milestone that looks appealing only when held up next to the alternative: dying before you even have a chance to get old—hardly a flattering comparison. Invariably, when I tell someone that I'm not looking forward to getting old, he or she is quick to reply, "It's better than the alternative."

Somehow, I find that to be a less-than-ringing endorsement. Surely we can do better. When faced with a life-or-death decision, who *wouldn't* choose life over that other not-so-great option? I'm sure that I could learn to live without a much-beloved appendage or two if I knew for certain that death was my only option. "Go ahead," I would tell my surgeon without hesitation. "Do what you must. As long as I can ... stay alive."

With death in the picture, a lot of otherwise unappealing options start to look downright rosy. The only exception to this rule is in cases where patients are considered brain-dead and placed on life support. Many people now choose a DNR (do not resuscitate) clause in their living will, indicating that resuscitation should not be attempted. Presumably, should they suffer a stroke or other traumatic event that could leave them catatonic or brain dead, they would rather end their lives than survive in a vegetative state.

I also detect this subtle problem that we have with the terminology. I've noticed that the term "old age" itself has a truly bad connotation. The problem is that stepping up to "old age" doesn't have the implication of simply moving on to the next stage of life, the stage immediately following middle age. It sounds more like the end of the line, the last stop, a holding cell where we all go to wait for the inevitable. We're not nervous about continuing on to the next phase of life; we just don't like the way we feel when we contemplate getting old. We've just know that sooner or later—probably more sooner than later—some spoilsport is going to come running into the room singing: "Turn Out the Lights; the Party's Over."

When we think of old age, most of us have the worst-case scenario in mind. We assume that we won't have all of our faculties. We worry about senility and losing our bodily functions and having to wear a device that looks and performs way too much like a big diaper. Worst of all, we dread the possibility that we'll spend our last years wasting away in a home for the aged. Yes, when we think of old age many of us wonder if an old-age home could be far behind.

I'm sure that just about every middle-aged person has some nightmarish vision, whether justified or not, of what our final years would be like in a nursing facility or "rest home." When my father could no longer give his mother the care she needed and was forced to put her into such an environment, I remember how she fought it tooth and nail. Getting her to the home was more like a covert mission than a transfer of belongings, not unlike trying to coax your pet cat into one of those carriers for trips to the vet.

My grandmother had no idea that she was going until we showed up at her door. I'm surprised that we didn't synchronize our watches and arrive in boats from the river wearing wet suits or show up in camouflage and rappel down from the roof with ropes.

On the morning that she was scheduled to depart, it took three hours of intense coaxing from a bevy of determined family members to convince her that leaving her home of sixty years was in her best interest. Her husband of forty-five years, my grandfather, had long since passed away. She could no longer be left alone to cook or bathe herself, and she had already fallen down a flight of stairs and broken her hip with no one in the house to assist her. Fortunately, she was able to summon the help of a neighbor on this occasion by yelling out of an open window. Her house had also been broken into on more than one occasion, and one of her caregivers had taken advantage of her, making this move a necessity.

Make no mistake, Mabel Robinson was a very independent woman and as tough as they came. When describing his mother's disciplinary style, my father has always depicted her as a "puncher" as if describing a Joe Louis–Max Schmeling fight. "Boy, my mother was a puncher," he says, balling up his fist and punching downward in a pile-driving motion. In reality, I presume he means in lieu of a spanker or a wild, open-hand slapper.

When my father took her car keys from her at age eighty because she was no longer safe to be behind the wheel of a car, she practically demanded that he step outside and settle the matter. This is a woman who, at the age of seventy-five, threatened to behead the next-door neighbor with a clothesline prop. I believe her exact words were—excuse my language—"I'll knock your goddamn head off!"

During a trip to a local grocery store, she grabbed the manager by his tie and yanked him into submission when he refused to honor an in-store special. I'm not sure what she said to this gentleman, but knowing her history and her pet terms, I would guess it was something like "Now you listen here …"

She never really forgave my father for taking this beloved automobile away. "J. J.," she said mournfully, "I don't know which I miss more, that car or Franklin (her late husband, my grandfather)." As she got older, I think the car was actually edging into the lead.

So you can imagine, headstrong woman that she was, how she resisted this necessary move with every fiber of her being. As my wife began preparing packing her things and preparing her for her new digs behind the scenes, I stood by and watched in horror as my father did the dirty work. The conversation went something like this:

"J. J.," she demanded from my father, "you mean you're taking me to a home?"

"Yes," he said simply.

"You mean right now!"

"Yes!" he insisted. "It's all ready for you. It's a beautiful place. You can't stay here anymore."

"I never thought that I would ever end up in a *home!*" She uttered the word home with the utmost of contempt.

"Come on, let's go," he said with false sense of finality.

"You mean we're going now …?" she said for a second time. Did I mention that she was suffering from dementia?

"Yes, I have a place ready for you."

"You mean I have to go to a home?"

And so it went. This little loop continued for at least an hour until my father, knowing his mother's desire not to have her neighbors see her removed from her home in shackles, played his trump card: "If you don't come with us right now, I'm going to call the police and have you taken out." He gave me a wink. The rest is history.

Hey, say what you will. We did the best we could. I only ask that you not consider our approach unkind. If you had known her, you would know that this was the only way to go about it.

When it comes to old-age homes, I don't think that my grandmother's attitude was too far from the norm. Despite the fact that there are many people living comfortable lives in some very nice facilities, we think of these residences as a death sentence rather than an alternative. It doesn't matter what we call them. A "senior retirement community" that features "independent living" is still a home.

My personal nightmare is probably typical. I visualize myself sitting alone, wasting away in Shirley's Personal Care Home, watching *The Price is Right* hosted by a 120-year-old Bob Barker, re-introducing myself to my senile friends on an hourly basis, drooling all over my nightshirt, sitting in my own excrement, and wondering exactly when it was that my children last paid me a visit. I would probably be wondering what their names were, for that matter. "Let's go, Mr. Robinson!" I can hear a nurse screaming into my good ear. "We don't want to miss out on wheelchair aerobics, do we?" Sound familiar?

So how can we maintain a positive outlook in the face of such negative publicity? How can we envision old age as a station we've earned, an honorable position in life, when we continue to see it in the worst possible light?

If these images aren't enough, I also detect a problem with heightened visual acuity; that is, old age is a little too easily recognized. No speculation necessary, we can see exactly what's coming. We have more than a notion of what could be waiting for us at the next level. We have a spectacular view from here, and, if you ask me, that's the whole problem.

Fighting the Effects of Gravity

I Can't Bear to Watch

When it comes to old age, I find that actual, physical documentation abounds. Once we hit midlife, vivid scenes from our not-too-distant future seem to manifest themselves in present-day form. Just like we don't have to wonder what WWII was like because of all of the footage taken during the conflict, we don't have to guess what old age is like because visible proof, real-life photographs of what we could be in for in our sixties and seventies, is there before us in black and white. If you're anything like me, you see the evidence on a daily basis. Like the family outings where there is simply too much food to eat, I think that sometimes we simply have too much proof at hand. When it comes to old age, very little is left to the imagination.

More times than I would care to mention, my wife and I have innocently traversed a two-lane stretch of highway only to find ourselves stranded behind an elderly couple motoring along at about half the legal speed limit. We can even tell from our vantage point behind them that they're up there in terms of age. Older individuals stereotypically seem to maintain a two-hands-on-the-wheel driving position at all times, and the driver, usually a male often sitting so low he barely see over the steering wheel, can be identified by the signature ball cap.

Although my spouse and I may sit in silence, gritting our teeth in frustration, we are each well aware of the futuristic implications. If we weren't, one of us would not invariably look at the other and say, "That will be us in twenty years."

My wife has even seen fit to add a twist to this little plot. When she sees an elderly woman driving an elderly male, presumably because he is no longer fit to drive, she now prognosticates: "Take a look at the future. You'll be out of it (she makes a distorted senile face, a glazed look with the tongue hanging out of an opened mouth for effect), and I'll have to chauffeur you around." Is this really necessary?

My father has even been quoted as saying on several occasions, "If I ever get like that," referring to an obviously pitifully senile individual, "put me away!" I usually tell him that I'll be more than happy to oblige.

To make matters worse, I often find myself avoiding banks and grocery stores on the first of the month because I know that the elderly will be out in force on that day. I don't mean to be insensitive, but it just seems that checkout lines are predictably slower and traffic around the stores is considerably more congested on the days when those on fixed incomes have received their monthly allotments of cash.

Couple these images with the frightening notion that there is just too much documentation, too many incriminating photographs, lying around. Hey, I'm not stupid. I see pictures of my parents when they were young. I see what they look like now. I see photos of myself as a crisp, wrinkle-free twenty-year-old. I find myself saying, "Damn, that kid looks good!" I have mirrors; I can see myself now. We were a close-knit family. My grandfather was always taking pictures of me and his five other grandchildren as well as his children with his state-of-the-art—at that time—Polaroid Land Camera during evening get-togethers. It seemed like fun at the time—to witness the miracle of pictures

Fighting the Effects of Gravity

developing before your eyes—but now I see things differently. I am convinced he took far too many revealing snapshots in the fifties. Why must there be so much damning evidence?

One particularly disturbing photo taken of my immediate family by a professional photographer some forty-three-years ago comes to mind. I was a mere fifteen-year-old, fuzzy-faced youth. My father was thirty-nine and my mother thirty-seven. In this photo opportunity, taken on the day that my father was receiving a prestigious award, I now, a painful four decades later, can never undo that cherub-faced, angelic visage. My father, now eighty-three, looks not only younger in the photo than he looks now but younger than *I look now*; and my mother, now eighty-one, bears a striking resemblance to the child star Shirley Temple. We not only left a paper trail, we left a photogenic paper trail. What can you say in the face of such data?

Even if there were no visible signs of aging, the alleged physical pain and suffering associated with old age, which in my case shouldn't come into play for another twenty-five to thirty years, can be all too easily predetermined. There's no guesswork here. My current formula for forecasting these infirmities is simple—it will probably get worse. Listen, I'm trying to remain positive, but I can put two and two together. I'm no stranger to the law of diminishing returns. Good wines may improve with age; aging humans tend to develop arthritis.

I would have to say that, given this philosophy, my outlook is shaky at best. Traditional wisdom indicates that by the year 2025: 1. My muscles will have atrophied to the point where they refuse to offer even token resistance to falling organs. 2. My teeth and gums, not in the greatest shape at this writing, will have given way to some brand of artificial chewing device. 3. My aching joints will prove to be a far more accurate barometer of approaching weather systems than they are even now.

But I can bring to light an even more troublesome example. It seems that even a live shot of my living parents can be a scary sneak peek at my future. For with each and every glance, I realize that, one day, I will have no choice but to gracefully assume their role. By means of a natural metamorphosis, my wife and I will eventually step into the shoes of our elders, and my children must, without protest, accept our baton.

Oh, my offspring will throw up their hands to avoid acceptance in a futile gesture, a motion similar to the one that the NBA players make to avoid being whistled for a foul. There won't be an official ceremony or coronation to mark the event, but it will happen. We'll all just look in the mirror one day and gasp, "Oh-mah-God, I've turned into my father" or mother, whichever the case may be.

It's similar in concept to the outgoing Miss America relinquishing her crown to the new titleholder—out with the old and in with the new; it's just the way things work. I'm beginning to enjoy trips to the grocery store. I get particularly upset when an announcement for a spill on aisle five interrupts one of my favorite songs on the PA. Yes, even as we speak, I feel myself turning into an entirely new species, an elderly creature known only as Mr. Robinson!

Case in point: When I was younger, I used to take great pleasure in informing my mother and father that I had rooms reserved for them at a certain state-operated nursing facility and that, when the need arose, I could have these rooms readied at a moment's notice. Indeed, at the first sign of any mental deterioration on their part—repetition of facts or stories, objecting too strenuously to loud music, getting too much pleasure out of a trip to the grocery store—they would be history.

They must have taken me somewhat seriously, too, because not long afterward they purchased a long-term care policy to cover them in case the need should arise. While you might deem this practice to be rubbing it in a bit, I was only kidding (for the most part). And besides, it kept them on their toes.

But times have changed. I now find myself in the same unenviable position. I see my own children poised to take my place. I hear them condemning my music. I hear the whispers about my lack of taste in clothing. I hear them comparing my freestyle dance movements—meant as harmless, in-house entertainment

Fighting the Effects of Gravity

only—to my father's. It's not a kind comparison; he does this strange move poking wildly in the air with two index fingers reminiscent of the Andrews Sisters high on crack cocaine.

I hear strangers and family alike calling me Mr. Robinson and "sir," and it gives me the creeps. With the advent of a new generation, my name has been officially changed to "Pap-pap." And though I had a hand in picking the title, I had no choice but to accept the crown.

Call me paranoid, but I remember hearing my oldest daughter and her ex-boyfriend talking as if I weren't in the room. Oh, it was quite a few years back, but it seems like yesterday. I heard them casually discussing the humane way to put one's parents in a home. "No," I distinctly my daughter's boyfriend say in rebuttal to her statement, "you can't put them in different homes; you have to put them both in the same home. You can't split them up like that." You would think he was discussing a litter of cats.

I've read this book from cover to cover. I know what comes next. It's only a matter of time. Just knowing that my own flesh and blood could turn the tables on me has forced me to squelch my menacing rhetoric toward my parents.

Not to mention the fact that my wife won't cut me a break. She insists on giving me grief, rubbing my nose in it, reminding me that I'm not a kid anymore. Recently, I asked her if I could still wear a Coogi sweater that I had in my wardrobe. "What's the difference," she replied. "You're old."

Her favorite means of gauging a person's age has become: "He's just a baby." "He's still young." "He's not so young anymore." And, "Oh, he's Daddy's age."

James Robinson Jr.

Go Forth in Peace

Despite our perceptions of the aging process, I think we can get over this old-age hang-up if we put our minds to it. I'm willing to go halfway. I can be realistic. I know better than to think that we middle-agers will ever be enthusiastic about growing old. There's no doubt that muscles atrophy as one ages, that voices get a little weaker, and that hair gets grayer and thinner as we age.

But let's not be totally put off by the negativity of the term "old age." Work with me on this. We'll be better off if we try to gain some perspective during these middle years. It's important that we don't psyche ourselves out at this stage of the game, before we really know what life will be like in twenty or so years. We should keep in mind that everyone's situation is different. We shouldn't paint the elderly with one wide brush. Let's not assume that we'll be totally incapacitated, unable to walk, talk, chew, or have any type of sexual contact without assistance.

The fact is, despite all of the negative scenarios that we envision for ourselves, I see individuals in their seventies and eighties who haven't missed a beat. I often hear that yesterday's age thirty is today's age fifty. I observe the so-called "elderly" living vital lives, doing everything at seventy-five that they did at forty-five: swimming, jogging, running marathons, and lifting weights. I was particularly surprised when I discovered how many seventy-five-year-olds are sexually active—with or without a medicinal erectile enhancer. Who's to say that we won't be among this group?

I also have to admit that old age looks pretty good on a lot of us. Tina Turner looks fabulous dancing on six-inch high heels at age seventy; Sean Connery is still getting leading-man roles at eighty, often romancing leading ladies half his age; and the late George Burns looked pretty good even when he hit the century mark. The—now deceased—Ronald Reagan was a robust sixty-seven when he ran for president for the third time (as you'll recall, he lost his first bid).

Fighting the Effects of Gravity

   The late James Brown—known as the "hardest-working man in show business"—was still singing and dancing until he died at seventy-three on Christmas Day of 2006. Chuck Berry performs to live audiences at eighty-four and no doubt still manages to execute that signature duck walk maneuver he made famous while playing the guitar. Hugh Hefner, the original "playboy," is still partying at the Playboy Mansion and entertaining playmates at eighty-five. And William Shatner—Captain Kirk himself; long removed from his *Star Trek* gig and making us laugh in *Priceline* ads—looks pretty good at eighty in his own right. So maybe they've had a tuck and cut and a lift here and there—more power to 'em.
   Closer to home, my mother, her living siblings, and my father all look great for their ages. I must admit that, in general, people don't look their ages anymore. I'm often surprised when I learn that someone is sixty-five or seventy years old. Maybe it's because I'm getting closer to that age. Last but not least, I know that I'll look pretty darned good at an advanced age, despite what my kids say.
   I've also seen older individuals who are obviously fading fast during these years. Watching someone you admire decline before your eyes is not an enjoyable experience. But I also see middle-aged individuals who look as if they too are sinking at a rapid clip. I watch reunion shows featuring actors and actresses from hit TV shows of the seventies and eighties, and it's a real shock to the system. I barely recognize these beloved characters in their middle-aged shells. All I can say is, "Oh my God, what happened to him/her?" Child actors who disappear from the scene and then reappear thirty years later for one reason or another are particularly susceptible to time-warp shock. I won't mention any names; let's just say a fading body plays no favorites.
   So let's try a new philosophy. Let's think of "old age" as our later years, as the next phase, not our final years. Think of it as a new beginning. Keep in mind the French proverb: "Forty is the old age of youth, but fifty is the youth of old age." If fifty is the youth of old age, sixty is just a notch above. We've just moved on to the next level. It's all in how you look at it. Think positive

thoughts and plan ahead in midlife to give yourself the best shot at a healthy life in these "later years."

Lay the groundwork today that will provide you with the best chance for a productive life past sixty. You know the drill: stay active, eat low-fat, healthy meals, lay off the cigarettes, watch the stress, and don't spend too much time in the sun. Like others in our age group, you might even pay a visit to a plastic surgeon for a little touch-up here and there if it will make you feel better. Think positive thoughts. Prepare physically, financially, and spiritually for what you know is likely in later life and hope for the best.

It would be nice if we were somehow rewarded for all of our hard work when old age becomes a reality. It would be great if we knew for certain that we would be on easy street and that we could just cruise happily through the remainder of our lives when we reach the road markers of sixty-five and seventy. We all know that's not going to happen. There's no chance of our bodies somehow being magically restored to their original splendor at a certain age.

I'm still not thrilled with the prospect of getting old, but I see enough people who are thriving in the latter stages of their life that I can at least maintain a positive outlook. What the heck, take the free bus rides and the senior citizen discounts; they come with the territory. Realize that growing old is not a death sentence; it's a necessary fact of life, and we are indeed lucky if we reach our "golden years." After all, you didn't have to make it this far. Relax. Make the best of it. As my surgeon said to me during my six-month checkup following colon surgery, "Just live your life."

In plain words, let's not worry about what could happen when we get old. There's no guarantee at any age. Keep in mind that you really don't have much choice in the matter and that getting old really *is* better than the alternative.

And, by the way, try not to use that term "old age."

It'll just bum you out.

Chapter 13: What Do You Mean I Have to Die?

*It's not that I'm afraid to die. I just don't
want to be there when it happens.*
        Woody Allen

WHAT'S WITH THIS DEATH thing, anyway? I mean, why has the thought of dying become such a factor with me all of a sudden? I must admit that now that I have reached my middle years, I'm seeing death in a much different light. I'm finding that the once inconsequential subject of taking my final breath has taken on much greater implications.

It seems that once I hit forty, the news that everyone ceases to breathe at one point or another—which gave me little cause for concern prior to midlife—has become a definite reality. Death has become, at least for me, a much more relevant proposition.

Suddenly, I have a much greater respect for the nonliving. It seems that every time a human being—especially a fellow middle-ager—reaches their expiration date, my ears perk up. I get that little anxious feeling. My once devil-may-care attitude toward death and dying—best summarized by the famous Alfred E. Neuman line, "What, me worry?"—can now be summed up in one startling declaration: "Hey, that could be me!"

James Robinson Jr.

Okay, I admit it. I'll shoulder the brunt of the blame. Maybe I didn't take death as seriously as I should have in my younger days, but I had my reasons. Mainly, I was brash and naïve, just too dumb to grasp that tired old adage about all good things coming to an end. Why should I have thought that my number would ever come up? I didn't think that I had a number. I was Superman prior to his first bout with Kryptonite, Samson before he fell asleep in Delilah's barber chair. I was untouchable, invincible, bullet proof. I was, for all intents and purposes, beyond the reach of death.

When I drive through the streets that surround a gothic, landmark structure known as the Cathedral of Learning on the campus of the University of Pittsburgh, I am always amazed by the young students who negotiate these streets with no fear, walking in front of moving cars as if, as my mother would say, they have "steel bumpers on their butts." Of course, it's also not beneath her to chastise them or anyone else who foolishly crosses in front of her car with reckless abandon. It is during these stressful times that she espouses what has become my favorite quote: "Step out and meet Jesus!"

"Look at them," I usually comment when I encounter these devil-may-care rascals. "They don't think that they can die."

I now realize that, to keep death at arm's length in those days, I often laughed off the whole notion of dying. I threw out clever little euphemisms when I heard that some unfortunate character had moved on merely as a way to keep death off my trail. I was often heard to remark that certain unlucky souls had "kicked the bucket" or "bought the farm" or that poor departed so-and-so would be "taking a dirt nap" for all eternity.

Even if someone near and dear to me died, like a favorite aunt or uncle or grandparent, I never took it too personally. I grieved in my own youthful, fanciful way, but I bounced back in a hurry. I recall attending my grandfather's wake and taking my first look at him in his casket. Although I was sad and shaken at the outset, I tried to make the best of it.

I was there in my parents' house when my grandfather slipped away, and I saw the look on his face. When I saw how his frail,

Fighting the Effects of Gravity

somewhat tortured eighty-year-old visage had been transformed to look thirty years younger in death by the skilled mortician, I seized the moment. I calmed my apprehensions by telling my relatives, "This isn't Papa. This is Sidney Poitier. We must be in the wrong room."

No, they weren't offended; they're used to these types of comments by now. Things were simple then. I figured, why belabor the point? They were dead, and I wasn't. I wasn't interested in reading the fine print. I wasn't even curious as to why they passed on. Something they ate, maybe. Some tragic defect in workmanship, perhaps.

Now I see the pendulum swinging my way, and my thinking has definitely been altered. Suddenly, the fine line that separates walking on earth and lying six feet beneath it doesn't seem quite so pronounced anymore. For a person who considered himself immortal for the first half of his life, this is a bit hard to take. It's not as if I think I'll go tomorrow; it's just that I didn't think that I would go at all. No doubt about it, we're both on the same page, me and death, and it's a bit of a sobering experience.

Mortality, all things considered, is definitely a drag. Here's what I mean:

Point #1: Cemeteries—I can't help but notice that cemeteries, which at one time represented no more to me than a parcel of land cluttered with headstones, have become a concept with which I can definitely relate. Yes, even though I've ridden in my share of funeral processions (with those little magnetic funeral-director flags attached to my fender), acted as pallbearer and assisted in the toting of my share of caskets, and stood in cemeteries probably dozens of times during burials, I never made the connection. No epiphanies. No light bulbs. No defining moments. Never once did I drop what I was doing and declare, "I need to prepare myself. One day, this is going to happen to me." Now it seems that I can't drive by a graveyard without picking a favorite spot, relating it to my own circumstances, and in general, sizing up the landscape for future reference.

Point #2: Bonding with the Obituaries—I also seem to have developed this genuine fascination with the obituaries. Although I had no interest in reading about recently deceased individuals prior to middle age, examining death notices has somehow become a daily ritual. No longer content to just peruse the sports and magazine sections, I am now willing to wade through a sea of eighty- and ninety-year-old attrition victims just to catch a glimpse of any middle-aged colleagues who may have unexpectedly cashed in their chips in the preceding twenty-four hours. I even get a little testy when the ages of the deceased aren't mentioned or when the manner of death is conspicuously absent. I guess you could call this behavior fear of death by association.

Though I may feel a trace of guilt, I usually end up rejoicing in the fact that I am not listed among them. As one older gentleman once said to me: "I read the obituaries every morning, and if my name isn't there, I drink my coffee."

Point #3: Please don't say "natural causes"—How a person dies has become paramount. It makes me feel a little better these days if each death is extraordinary. In fact, I get the weirdest feeling when I hear that a fellow middle-ager has died an absolutely *unextraordinary* death; yes, left this earth a confirmed victim of *natural causes!* Queue the *Jaws* music: Dunta, Dunta, Dunta ... For some reason, this term seems to push a whole row of my middle-aged buttons. I find myself rooting for some type of asterisk, hoping that every death be linked to some extenuating circumstance, which somehow makes it a little easier to stomach.

Fighting the Effects of Gravity

For instance, have you ever found yourself breathing a sigh of relief when you noticed that a fellow midlifer had perished while doing something questionable, such as swimming or surfing in shark-inhabited waters? I remember watching a news story in which a surfer had had an unfortunate run-in with a great white shark. As you might imagine, the surfer got the worst of it. The only evidence of this encounter was a surfboard with a humongous chunk removed and a shredded wetsuit.

I've often heard experts say that from the shark's vantage point, looking up at the surfer on the surface of the water (they often attack from below their victim), flat on the board with his arms and legs flailing about in the water—the typical position of a surfer who is going out to catch a wave—the surfer looks like a seal or some other tasty, meaty delicacy through the eyes of the infamous species *Chondrichthyes*.

These so-called authorities usually go on to say that sharks don't consider humans a delicacy because our bodies consist of more bone than meat. For this reason, these experts insist, most discriminating sharks will take one bite, sample the flesh, as it were, realize they made a mistake, and let us go. Just one bite, eh?

James Robinson Jr.

A bite for a shark could be one fairly sizable chunk of humanity for us—more like the pound of flesh that Shakespeare's Shylock character spoke of in *Hamlet*. But then again, rather comforting in a Julia Child sort of way. Anyway, this particular shark apparently wasn't very cultured.

Well, if you're anything like me, a death such as this probably leaves you unfazed. It's not that we don't have sympathy for the surfer; it's just that we know that we would never expose ourselves to such a degree of danger. Fact is, these surfer dudes know that there are twenty-foot carnivores with two rows of serrated-jagged teeth, questionable eyesight, finicky menus, and never-ending appetites lurking in the water when they start flopping around making themselves look like hors d'oeuvres. They ignore the danger for the sake of a great wave. As the cartoon hero Underdog used to say, "He knew the job was dangerous when he took it."

So we put it out of our minds. Admit it; you don't give these reports a second thought. I know I can think of one very basic rule to avoid such an unfortunate end: if there are predators the size of stretch limos in the water incapable of distinguishing between a fun-loving human being and a mammal with whiskers and fins, don't go in!

I've also heard tell of a poor gent who met his untimely end while jogging in Yellowstone Park on a path that was apparently a little too close to a mother grizzly and her cub. Once a year, I shake my head in amazement at the people who venture to Spain and don't return because they chose to run that silly race with the bulls. Once again, fatalities like these are easy to explain away. *Tough break,* I say to myself, *but I don't jog in areas frequented by protective one-thousand-pound bears, and I know better than to try to outrun a group of frenetic bulls.* So why give it a second thought?

While I can easily dismiss these deaths as acts of questionable judgment, plain-old natural causes makes me nervous. The situation has gotten to the point where just hearing this term makes me a little uncomfortable. In the years to come, I worry that the utterance of this phrase will send me into a full-blown

Fighting the Effects of Gravity

frenzy, something similar to the infamous Three Stooges "Niagara Falls" skit. You remember, don't you, "Slo-o-o-wly, I turn ..."?

Oh sure, while many of you may equate this cause of death with a heart attack or a stroke and think nothing of it, I dwell on the more subtle implications. These types of fatalities are just a little too easy to line up with my own situation—death by association all over again. I'm thinking, if it can happen to him or her, it can happen to me.

From my angle, there's something about a forty-year-old man breathing his last breath while performing a seemingly mundane task that lays it all on the line. Even my aging mind can connect the dots. I figure, he's forty, he keeled over while merely attempting to shovel snow from his walk. I'm fifty-eight (a full eighteen years his senior), and I have performed this task on many occasions. Sl-o-o-o-o-wly, I turn ...

Point #4: I am not alone—There's also something about my wife's recent behavior that leads me to believe that she and I are of an identical mind-set. I say this because when stricken with any ailment more serious than a hangnail, she often quotes liberally from her always moving "when I die" speech.

Flipping quickly through the section that urges me to remarry, she struggles to make one point perfectly clear: that shipping her remains to the mortuary owned by her ex-boyfriend would constitute a post-life insult of the highest order, apparently a fate far *worse* than death. She is quite adamant about this issue. If she's told me once, she's told me a hundred times, "Don't take me to (funeral director's name)!"

My wife recently informed me of a dream she had the night before in which she, her mother, and the aforementioned funeral director were in this particular gentleman's funeral home watching a scary movie on television. (I told you it was a dream.) At one point, she remembers saying, "I told Jay (my nickname) not to bring me here!" I tell you, she's serious about this.

Such a grievous error, don't you see, would grant this gentleman license to view her once-girlish figure in the raw in all of its middle-aged splendor. Dead or alive, the embarrassment would be beyond words. "I've had three children!" I'm sure she would desperately want to inform him. Let's face it, none of us looks like we did twenty years ago.

Point #5: How may I leave here? Dare I count the ways?—It also has dawned on me in recent years that there are, in fact, far too many ways to meet one's fate in this complicated, high-tech society. In addition to the ever-increasing likelihood of a violent vehicular crash—plane, car, train, boat, motorcycle, bicycle, jet ski, mountain bike, skateboard, roller blade—simply being in the wrong place at the wrong time can, all too often, gain one a quick audience with his or her maker.

I've seen a tragic number of innocent souls of all ages lose their lives in the crossfire of a gangland shootout or while playing a game of golf that just happened to be interrupted by a thunderstorm. I watched Jim Brady get gunned down in 1981 for simply standing too close to President Reagan during an assassination attempt. Governor John Connelly suffered the same fate while merely sitting beside JFK in the famous limousine in Dallas in 1963. Secret Service agents know what they're getting into. Besides, they receive fairly sizable salaries and benefits to deal with such hazardous duty. White House press secretaries and unwary Texas governors, it seems to me, should be exempt from the carnage.

I also wonder about the fortunes of someone who just happens to be buying stamps during a visit from a disgruntled postal worker or a 7-Eleven employee who is unlucky enough to be working the night shift when some desperate, spaced-out bozo decides to take what little money may be in the cash register and shoot the night clerk on the way out. I see some brave employees fighting back, but the danger is all too real. I have come to realize that these are all situations that can easily lead to a quick and untimely exit.

Oh, yeah, I know. The likelihood of some of these events occurring during your lifetime isn't very high. After a recent plane crash, I heard that your odds of becoming a fatality in a major airline disaster are, in fact, quite low, something in the area of one

Fighting the Effects of Gravity

in ten million. If you think about it, we can go two or more years without seeing a major commercial plane crash in the United States. Flying in an airplane is, I keep hearing, much safer than driving a car. Think about it. What were your chances of being on any of the hijacked planes that met their fateful end on September 11, 2001? (The odds of winning the Powerball, by the way, are about 1 in 200,000,000.) Doesn't it just figure that the odds for cashing in are much worse than the odds for cashing out?

The July 25, 2000, crash of a Concorde Jetliner in France bears this out. This deadly accident was the first mishap of any kind for this supersonic jet in their twenty-seven years of flying. The Concorde flew its last flight in 2003—unfortunate in my book. The way I see it, we should have been falling over each other to ride this speedy airliner. Heck, with these odds, we should have been lining up to fly supersonic transportation every day. We should have been jumping on supersonic jets to fly at twice the speed of sound (1,500 mph) to the local convenience store to pick up a Slushie and bag of chips.

Then again, the $9,500 airfare and the aging fleet of planes no doubt had a lot to do with its demise and could have been a bit of a deterrent. I find these types of statistics somewhat comforting, but I still get a little queasy every time I climb aboard a projectile that soars to thirty thousand feet and slices through the air at five hundred mph.

James Robinson Jr.

How Will It Happen?

If you're anything like me, you've already begun to ponder the burning question: "How will I die?" Yes, with death now such a powerful reality, I can't help but speculate about what will take me out of circulation; how might I take my final bow? It's a very thought-provoking question, made more difficult by the fact that I may never know the answer. Death could identify itself in the form of some protracted disease and take its time to happen or could come in a moment.

I sometimes wonder, will I die quickly? You know the "He never saw it coming, never knew what hit him" type of death? My father likes to joke about the guy who gets squashed by a falling piano and how lucky the survivors would be because they wouldn't have the expense of a full-size casket. He's definitely seen his share of *Road Runner* cartoons.

Although I felt a terrible sense of loss when they were killed, I found it somewhat comforting when I heard that John F. Kennedy Jr., his wife, and her sister died instantly when their plane struck the water near Martha's Vineyard in 1999. It's unfortunate that they lost their lives at such a young age, but there is something to be said for going fast.

Think about it. Would you want to die young, quickly, and relatively painlessly, or live thirty years longer and go out suffering, living for months or years with death as a constant companion, knowing full well what's destined to happen? A friend of mine once told me that he would just like to "wake up dead one day."

I think many people might take the long route due to the fact that, despite the suffering, you would want to live as long as possible, savoring every moment no matter how painful the end may be. The notion of living as long as possible might be upheld when a hostage, held at gunpoint, gets into a car with his or her abductor rather than refusing to comply as is suggested. Although fear plays a part, the desire for self-preservation kicks in and the

Fighting the Effects of Gravity

victim is willing to do whatever is necessary to extend his or her life.

I think I'd opt for the piano at this stage of my life. I've watched people go out suffering, and it's as painful to watch for the family as it is painful for the victim. Dying with haste also means you won't have time to obsess about what's coming—unless, of course, you consider that "life flashing before your eyes" phenomenon.

Granted, just knowing that your plane is about to crash twenty-three seconds before impact, which was the case with a US Airways plane crash near Pittsburgh in 1994, would cause a *very long* and torturous twenty-three seconds, but twenty-three seconds nonetheless.

But I still have a problem with someone who can say unequivocally that an accident victim died "instantly." How can they be so sure? Unless they were there, how would they really know that death was instantaneous? If a terrorist drives a vehicle loaded with one hundred pounds of explosives into a military barracks and is delivered to Allah and the alleged seventy-two sexually primed virgins that await him in paradise in the ensuing explosion, there's little doubt about his fate. Believe it, he died instantly.

But there are marginal cases. I could imagine such an expert telling my family that I died instantaneously in a violent mishap to give them comfort. "Don't worry," the scholarly one would assure them, "he was killed instantly." Meanwhile, I would be the only one who knew the truth, who knew that while the impact may have made it appear that death was swift and painless, I suffered like the dickens for the better part of a minute and a half.

I also wonder if death will come very slowly—if some aggressive malignancy or unfriendly disease will provide that slow, lingering type of death. I've watched enough friends and relatives endure long, protracted, painful farewells to know that I'd rather not exit in this fashion. How many times have you seen a case where a man or woman takes his or her spouse's life because they begged him or her to end their suffering?

During the writing of this book, character-actor Richard Farnsworth committed suicide because he found it impossible to deal with the long-term pain associated with his illness. And need I resurrect the name of the (ironically) late Dr. Kevorkian?

On the other hand, death could simply come calling as I sleep. The sleep-and-never-wake-up option has always been a favorite of mine. Yes, dying without even having that dreadful twenty-three seconds to worry about sounds very good to me, at this point.

I even realize that death could come calling amid truly bizarre circumstances. After swallowing food for over fifty years with little difficulty, I could get some normally harmless morsel lodged in my throat with no one around to administer the Heimlich maneuver, for instance. Don't look at me like that. Stuff happens, you know.

Mulling over the infinite possibilities of my demise often shoves me over into the introspective side. I often get glimpses of death-related incidents—snapshots and images of occurrences gone by. Some happenings are humorous while others are very poignant, but all are indicative of how death touches us and becomes a part of our lives. I tend to reminisce about these incidents, personal stories, and situations that didn't seem very pertinent until I reached this age. Consider the following:

The "father-in-law and the hat" incident— I have this image of my late father-in-law wearing this mangled, wide-brim hat—he didn't realize that he had sat on it in the car on the way to the gravesite—as he struggles to break the fall of his grief-stricken sister. Her legs had suddenly become weak at the sight of her husband's casket being lowered into the ground.

Despite the sad overtones, I chuckle—okay, I laugh out loud—when I think about the unlikely sight of so large a man (five-foot eight-inches, 280 pounds) donning an Art Carney, *Honeymooners*-style crumpled hat to come to the aid of his overwrought sibling. Granted, I have a warped sense of humor, but you'll have to admit that there's a certain funny/sad dichotomy in the scene—a huge man in a crumpled sombrero assisting a grieving widow? I do feel a bit ashamed as I laugh, but I laugh anyway.

Fighting the Effects of Gravity

The "rain-soaked funeral" incident—Every once in a while, I get a vision of myself at age twenty-eight, flanked by five waterlogged cousins as we struggle, in a driving rainstorm, to transport my grandmother's casket up a steep hill to her final resting place. Other than the obvious romantic implications, this incident holds far more meaning for me at my near-sixty status than just the drenched three-piece suit I ruined during the foray to the grave. Consider it a form of payback.

For some reason, it now just seems apropos that we had to fight the elements and hilly terrain to bury this beloved woman, a highly revered figure who never hesitated to do battle for us over the years. A woman who enjoyed nothing more than being in the company of her four surviving children and thirteen grandchildren right up until the day she died at the age of eighty.

The "face of death" incident—Despite the fact that she passed away over twenty-five years ago, I sometimes get these discomfiting glimpses of my aunt's face the day before she died. I see her lying in her hospital bed, weighing an emaciated ninety-five pounds, eyes agape, mouth wide open, head pivoting mechanically from side to side in a futile attempt to recognize her family, having entered into the final conflict of a long, painful assault from rectal cancer.

My aunt lived with us on the third floor of my parents' spacious home during the final year of her life, and I had occasion to watch her slow decline. I even carried her to a waiting car for her final trip to the hospital, and it is this picture that sticks in my mind.

But I also remember how beautiful her face was in healthier times. I remember her spirit, how she refused to have the type of surgery that would have compromised her fastidious nature, how she beat the odds for two years, and how much she enjoyed life when she was living.

The "line through the parishioner" incident—I recollect laughing out loud at age ten when I noticed that my father, a Presbyterian minister, had drawn a line through the name of one of the sick-and-shut-in members of his congregation listed weekly in the church bulletin. I can still see the bulletin in question sitting in the console between the front seats of his car, where he used it as a reference when he visited the sick. Placing a check beside a sick parishioner's name I could understand, but crossing off a name seemed awfully suspicious.

Knowing the insensitive implication, that this crossed-out individual, this scratched-out child of God had, in fact, been officially removed from life's roster, I couldn't resist pulling his chain a bit. "I can't believe you did that," I said. "She died, and you crossed her name off the list. I guess that means you won't have to visit her anymore."

My father, now retired, vehemently denies these accusations on one hand but then jokingly threatens to scratch another person off his list if the time is right. In the spirit of "what goes around comes around," since my own name appeared on this same list while I recovered from colon surgery over fifteen years ago, you'll be happy to know that I don't find this anecdote quite so funny.

Where to Put It?

Having never died before, I have to ask myself: "What do I do with it?"—my own body that is; you know, my remains. It's probably the most difficult question I'll ever have to answer. After all, it's my own body, I'm attached to it, and here I am trying figure out how to dispose of it. The fact is that I form attachments easily. I was always devastated when we had to dispose of a family pet. My father always got stuck with the dirty work—having to make solo trips to the vet to have our dogs put down. To this day, one of my worst fears is standing in front of a veterinarian, staring at a doomed pet and crying like that little boy heading to Wichita, Kansas. What would that do to my staunch image?

Very few people know it, but I'm a very emotional person. I've just managed to keep it hidden all of these years. On one occasion, my father's eyes welled up with tears as our vet began preparing our family dog—a fifteen-year member of our family—for the inevitable. During the preparations, our long-time vet stopped to ask, "Do you want the leash?" These days, some pet owners even choose to hold their animals while they're being euthanized. No thanks; a kind send-off but too traumatizing for me.

So it only makes sense that I would agonize over the demise of living tissue that has been holding my liver, kidneys, bladder, and spleen in place. I don't have an appendix. When I had my Crohn's surgery, it was found to be missing—never raised its hand during roll call, as it were. No explanation was ever given.

I've been keeping this body healthy and clean for almost sixty years. I hate to think of it returning to dust, you know, that ashes-to-ashes thing. Not to mention the fact that trying to figure out what to do with it means that I'm no longer going to be using it—not a comforting thought; very distressing actually. After all, we're not talking about a used car here.

While I'm not at all anxious to broach this subject, I see three basic options: **1.** I could leave orders to hand over my body to the local crematorium; **2.** I could opt for the traditional burial; **3.** I could donate my body to science—a noble gesture if I do say so myself, which is, by the way, free.

I guess I would have to say that numbers 1 and 2 appear to be the frontrunners, but I'm not thrilled with either one. Truth be told, I have this dreaded fear of being buried alive, and I don't like the idea of being six-feet-under whether I'm dead or not. Yeah, I know, I won't know the difference, but for some reason I'm still not in love with the idea. I guess I'm thinking of death from a living man's perspective.

I've also heard of variations to these basic themes. I know that the ancient Egyptians, in addition to wrapping their dead, buried their deceased with their belongings because they were believed to be going on to another life. I remember that my grandmother wanted my grandfather to be buried in a casket with blue satin lining because it matched his eyes. When my father pointed out that this was a useless exercise because his eyes would be closed anyway, it was on. "Listen here, James Joseph," she said, "you know one thing; you don't know what you're talking about. Franklin had beautiful eyes. I don't see nothing wrong with Franklin's eyes matching that cloth. You're just a spoilsport." Once again, the matter almost ended up being settled in Ali–Frasier, Thrilla in Manilla fashion in the parking lot.

I know of elderly widows who have asked to be buried with their pets, romantic individuals who insist that their ashes be scattered on their favorite golf course, at sea, or off a windy cliff. One gentleman even requested that he be buried in his beloved Corvette. He purchased twelve burial plots for this purpose. His request was at first denied but was then granted by the cemetery. I know of one deceased person who, instead of the traditional casket viewing, was laid out sitting upright in a chair, wearing a dinner jacket and holding his favorite pipe in his teeth. I have also heard tell of a child whose dead body was placed on a tricycle for viewing. To each his own, but a bit sick if you ask me.

Then there's the ritual practiced by certain gang members who honor a slain "homey" by pouring a "forty"—a forty-ounce bottle of beer—on the grave. If I opt for a traditional burial,

Fighting the Effects of Gravity

perhaps a family-size bottle of Gatorade or a half-gallon carton of fruit punch drink splashed about my burial site would be more apropos. Although I'm really not too thrilled about any of the above options (the child on the tricycle sounds particularly unattractive), my decision now seems like a no-brainer.

I'm no big fan of cremation, but I must admit that I never cared much for the funeral-home scene. I dread the notion of allowing friends and family members to "view" my preserved remains or having someone actually proclaim how "good" I look in this final state. When I attend a wake with my family, we can hardly wait to get back to the car so that we can discuss the appearance of the corpse. He or she "didn't look too good" is often the consensus. We then rate the mortician and how well they did with what they had to work with.

I've also been on the other side. I've known times when my wife and other family members have gone in early before a viewing with a brush and a curling iron and worked on the remains of a deceased relative.

I now realize how silly this exercise is. Of course he or she didn't look good. He or she is no longer breathing. This is no beauty contest. It's bad enough that we critique the appearance of the living. Dead people traditionally don't look good. I'm sure it has something to do with the fact that the heart is no longer pumping blood to certain vital areas of their bodies. But I think we make these kinds of remarks because of the awkward situation that we're placed in. We don't know what to say.

We go to a funeral home to "pay our respects," which actually means paying our respects to the relatives of the deceased. After all, the dead person could care less. I mean, what can you say when you walk up to an ornate metal or wood container surrounded by flowers and look at the well-prepared carcass laid out inside? I mention a wood casket because I know of one family who buried their father in a cedar casket. I find this to be very unfortunate indeed. After all, it seems quite superfluous that this magnificent coffer will be covered with dirt and mold and I could have used it to store my wools.

James Robinson Jr.

For me, no matter how many wakes I attend, there's always that initial shock of seeing a lifeless corpse. If the person is a stranger, the very first thing that comes into my head is "Yep, they're dead all right. I wonder what they looked like alive?" Then I might take a closer look to check out the quality of the embalming. But the real question is, why am I looking? What good does it serve?

I sometimes carry on a conversation with the members of the deceased person's family who are standing around the casket. If it's a particularly tragic or somber occasion—and I have seen my share of those—I do a hit and run. Unless it's family, of course, I give the perfunctory "sorry for your loss" and hit the road. I've actually seen contentious verbal jousts take place in the vicinity of the casket itself—my own family included. Weddings and funerals tend to take on a life of their own, and when things get ugly, I don't want to be a part of that life. However, there have been times when a death is treated in a more upbeat fashion and there might even be some happy greetings, hugs, and laughter among family and mourners around the casket.

Despite the obvious good that it could do for humanity, I've heard about the pranks that pre-med students pull with cadavers that are donated for educational purposes—putting this body part here and that body part there. I once heard a story of a group of medical students who hung a body on the back of a door as a prank and frightened a custodian so badly that, when he saw it, he actually jumped out of a window. Luckily, it was a first-floor window. Call me vain, but I'll have to give a big thumbs-down to this proposal too.

Fighting the Effects of Gravity

Therefore, I have made my decision. Scattering my ashes from a windy precipice after a quick and painless death at a ripe old age without the shame of a suspect minister crossing my name off a church bulletin before rigor mortis has even set in, sounds like a keeper at the moment. I also plan to donate whatever parts of my body are still viable for organ donation. But don't hold me to it.

Cemeteries? Obituaries? Cremation? "Sl-o-o-o-wly I turn?" The Heimlich maneuver? Why the sudden interest in the hereafter? My guess is that my sudden preoccupation is death's way of saying, "Hello," like the Hawaiian beauties welcoming you to their country as you disembark from an airplane by putting one of those ceremonial leis around your neck. This death dude, apparently somewhat familiar with this endearing Hawaiian formality, has met me on the tarmac of life and slipped a lei over my head.

I have come to believe that these less-than-uplifting thoughts are simply a normal part of the growth process for someone in his mid- to late fifties. Having lost my youthful innocence, death has become a friend of sorts, a companion, but in all likelihood, a necessary reality. Apparently, the older you get, the closer the friendship grows. Midlife, which has sponsored my mental rebirth, has obviously introduced me to the notion that everyone has a time limit, that nothing or no one lives forever. I can't complain.

The jig is up, but I guess it's about time. I only wish I would have seen it coming.

It seems so sudden. One day I'm immortal, the next day I've got death in my BlackBerry. I don't mean to be flippant, but have I missed something? Perhaps memos were sent out to all middle-age inductees and mine was inadvertently lost in the shuffle, sent to the wrong address perhaps. No doubt, they went something like this:

> Hi! Welcome to middle age. Just a note to introduce myself and inform you that I'll be in the back of your mind from here on in. Don't worry, I won't be too obtrusive. See you soon. We'll do lunch. Have a nice day!

Your new friend,
Death
Death

The Wake-Up Call

I have come to realize that as unsettling an experience as it may seem to be, discovering one's mortality during the middle stages of life is a very necessary part of living. As weird as it may sound, it's not until we become totally cognizant of death that we are fully able to appreciate life. As the British novelist E. M. Forster once wrote: "Death destroys a man: the idea of death saves him." Based on my recent experience, an intimate, live-in relationship with death actually brings out the best in human beings. Like a well-fitting three-piece suit, death, in an odd way, looks pretty good on us.

Somehow, just getting in touch with our mortality, knowing that we're going to die, infuses us with new life. Once we realize that our lives could be snuffed out at any time—that our next breath could be our last—our lives change for the better. We tend to think a little more before we speak, we walk a little more before we run, we hold our loved ones a lot closer, and we treasure the moment like we never treasured it before. In a strange way, sensing our demise is a rite of passage, a ceremony marking our transition from youth to middle age. Somehow, this knowledge actually sets us free. We begin to view our lives from an entirely different perspective.

I bet you've noticed that, once the reality of death sets in, the small things that used to set you off don't bug you as much as they did before. You don't get so excited when the car won't start or when the dog does a number on the new carpet. Just knowing that you won't be around forever, I'll wager that your earthly goals of money and success don't have the same significance that they once did. Death has a certain calming effect. It's one situation that you can't negotiate with, talk to, or buy your way out of.

Once we realize that we're expendable, our priorities stack up much differently. I also detect a more philosophical approach to this whole fiasco. I catch fellow middle-agers espousing such profundities as "Don't sweat the small stuff; life is too short." "You can't take it with you." "Just take it one day at a time." Or the ever-popular "As long as you have your health."

I have also noticed that, with death in our thoughts, we place a higher premium on being happy. Happiness, for some of us, finally becomes our rightful, ultimate goal. We become so infatuated with the notion that we begin to toss the word around indiscriminately, as if it were part of some secret midlife code. How many times have you heard someone utter, "As long as he's *happy*" or "I just want you to be *happy*, dear" or "Sure, she has all of that money and fame, but is she really … *happy?*"

While many of us see life differently when confronted with the reality of dying, that doesn't stop many of us from fearing the inevitable. Despite the fact that I consider myself to be a spiritual person and I presume that there is some type of life for me after this one, I admit that I have this needless blind fear of dying, nonetheless. Perhaps it's the absolute finality of it all that makes me, and many others I have spoken to, skittish of the hereafter despite the anticipation of an afterlife.

I know of many individuals who were never able to accept the inevitable. I have heard that the famous actor Bela Lugosi, even with death imminent, kept repeating to those who sat at his bedside that he didn't want to die. No doubt this is the worst-case scenario, but it underscores the fact that we have to get ourselves in the proper frame of mind long before the end comes. Once we come to grips with the notion that everything, including human life, has a beginning and an end, we can hopefully avoid such unpleasant endings.

As mature individuals, I think we middle-agers have learned how to live; we just haven't quite figured out how to exit this life with grace. I sense that we simply aren't very comfortable with the fact that we have to die. We really don't want to talk about it. Magazine articles seldom broach the subject. (Could you imagine the headline "How to die with grace" mixed in with features on great skin, celebrity weddings, and a primer on how to have a magnificent orgasm?) I haven't come across too many books that dare to discuss the dreaded "D" topic either.

Fighting the Effects of Gravity

The fact is that we get a little too comfortable during our stay on earth. We forget that our time on this planet is fleeting, more like a lease than a buy. We grow attached to these bodies and don't like the idea that they'll eventually sputter and then stop working altogether. That dust-to-dust notion doesn't seem to thrill us in the least, either. The way I see it, we know how impractical it would be to live forever—we just don't like the idea of dying. Many of us haven't come to the conclusion that death is just a necessary part of life. We don't realize that dying is a natural event, merely the flip side of being born.

We should take heart in the knowledge that just as we all have to get old, we all have to die. There are no pardons or commutations of this death sentence. While you may witness someone get away with murder during your lifetime or get away with something else that you find grossly unfair, take solace in the fact that it will all even out in the end. Think of death as the great equalizer, the one big constant in life. "Sooner or later," as the Cher song goes, "we all sleep alone." There's no getting around it.

We also shouldn't let our heightened awareness of dying have a negative impact on the way we live. I can name any number of individuals who accomplished many things late in life and didn't let the fact that they were destined to die stand in the way of living.

I think of famous persons such as George Burns, who was in show business for over seventy-five years and performed on stage until he died in 1996 at the age of one hundred; golfer Arnold Palmer, who couldn't wait to resume hitting golf balls after his bout with prostate cancer; Pablo Picasso, who painted prolifically until he died at age ninety-two; and J. S. Bach, who continued to write choral works and fugues until he passed away in 1750 at the age of sixty-five. Singer Tony Bennett, enjoying a resurgence in popularity, can be heard crooning his trademark songs at age eighty-two. Erma Bombeck, one of my inspirations, continued to make us laugh until she died from complications following surgery in 1996.

But I think all of these people share a common bond—they obviously enjoyed or still enjoy their chosen professions. Further, I would wager that they are doing now or were doing during the course of their lives what they felt they were put on earth to do. They were, or are, simply too busy living meaningful lives and pursuing their passions to worry about dying. Apparently, there is very little time to fear death if you feel as if you are fulfilling your destiny on earth.

I recall watching an interview in 1991 with former Los Angeles Lakers star Magic Johnson not long after he was diagnosed as being HIV-positive. After he had gotten over the initial shock, I remember how surprised I was when I heard him say at his young age, "If I die tomorrow, I've had a good life." Having to deal with the prospect of death forced him to realize how good his life had been.

In terms of Magic's statement, I would have to say that, though I've had a good life in many ways, there are several things that I have yet to achieve. My writing career, for instance, is only just now starting to take shape. In terms of family—wife, children, mother, father, grandchildren and my extended family members of cousins and uncles—I couldn't be happier. I have the best children a father could ask for, two parents who love and support me, and a wife who affords me more love and respect than I probably deserve.

But in terms of career success, I hunger for more. I don't feel as if I ever quite hit the mark. Most of my dissatisfaction comes from the fact that I can only think of a few fleeting moments when I felt an inner satisfaction about what I was doing in the workplace. I think the problem was that I always went looking for the jobs when, in fact, the jobs should have come looking for me. If you find the right fit in terms of a job, it's not a job at all; it's a calling. So if I died tomorrow, I would be sad for what I hadn't accomplished. But that's in the past. I do feel as if I have a certain window to work with and I'm going to use the gifts that I have to make up for any time lost.

Fighting the Effects of Gravity

I think we all tend to gauge our lives in different ways, often in comparison to others' lives. Some people might look at some aspect of my life and consider me fortunate, while I might look at theirs and long for something that they have.

I am also reminded of several individuals who knew death was imminent but still managed to live their lives to the fullest right to the very end. I remember Senator Hubert Humphrey disembarking from an airplane, smiling and waving heartily to a crowd despite his gaunt appearance. He was suffering from an advanced stage of cancer at the time. At his funeral, Walter Mondale delivered a touching eulogy and ended by saying, "Senator Humphrey taught us how to live, and in the end, he taught us how to die."

I also recall John Wayne, the famous actor, appearing at the Oscar ceremonies prior to his death. Despite the fact that he was obviously wasting away from a terminal illness, he, too, remained upbeat. He managed a smile while standing at the podium to present an award, and what an inspiration it was to the viewing audience. Both men could have lived their final days in seclusion, away from the prying eyes of the public and media. But they chose to face death with purpose and resolve.

When the end comes, I can only hope that I'll be ready. My goal is to face it head on and with dignity. Though I may have misgivings now, I'm sure I'll accept it, just as I've learned to accept other obstacles I've faced throughout my life, situations over which I had no control. Hopefully, a calm will come over me like it did before my extensive surgery in 1996. I eventually realized that I had no power over my fate on the operating table, and I'm sure that I'll feel the same when the time comes.

I want sentiments similar to those expressed after the November 29, 2001, death of ex-Beatle George Harrison to be issued on my behalf. Harrison's family issued a statement that concluded, "He left this world as he lived it—conscious of God, fearless of death, and at peace, surrounded by family and friends."

I can only hope to meet my demise as bravely as the famous Sioux Indian Chief Crazy Horse. Prior to teaming up with Sitting Bull to ruin General George Custer's weekend at the Little Big

James Robinson Jr.

Horn in 1876, he was heard to say: "Hokahey! It's a good day to fight! It's a good day to die! Strong hearts, brave hearts to the front. Weak hearts and cowards to the rear!"

I'm hoping that I'll make the fearless Crazy Horse proud, that I'll be a brave heart. I'll put my life in God's hands and accept my fate when the time comes. When the final curtain begins to fall, I'm sure I'll realize that it's no big deal, that nothing is as ominous as it seems. As Winston Churchill once joked, "I am ready to meet my Maker. Whether my Maker is prepared for the ordeal of meeting me is another matter." If death comes quickly or in my sleep, all the better.

In a way, there is no better testimony to one's existence than to say the words, "I'm ready." Saying you're ready to die is not a death wish. In all likelihood, it means that you've accomplished all or most of what you set out to do. When you think about it, our lives are a mere stage. Our entire existences are spent in preparation for death. To quote Leonardo da Vinci: "While I thought I was learning how to live, I have been learning how to die." When you've said the words "I'm ready," there should be no funeral, only a celebration of a life lived with dignity and purpose.

In the final analysis, however, I think that middle age is actually much too late in the scheme of things to come to terms with the inevitable. With so many us fearful of death, we need to be subjected to constant reminders, bombarded with what could happen to us at any given point of this little program. Early in our lives, we need to begin to cultivate a healthy respect for death without fearing it. We need to get comfortable with the inevitability of it all without allowing it to take over our lives. Every creature, after all, is born into the world, and every creature, at some point, ceases to exist. We're no different. We want to get to know death without becoming intimate as early in the game as possible. We want to maintain a good working relationship with this death fellow without allowing him to set up housekeeping in our psyches.

To this end, we should be kept apprised of how tenuous life really is so that we can live each day in the proper frame of mind. Since watching fellow human beings suffering and dying by the thousands on the evening news has become routine, I think that a more direct approach is essential.

Just think of how great it would be if we could no longer avoid the realities of death until it is too late, when it is practically staring us in the face. What if we had a daily reminder, a wake-up call? What if we all had our own personal messenger to hand-deliver the edict to us each and every morning? Is that so far-fetched? We have personal trainers and cooks, live-in nannies and housekeepers, spiritual gurus, financial advisors, and valets. So why not someone to convey this important message on a daily basis?

In the true spirit of a no-nonsense boot camp, I envision each of us with our very own, marine-like drill sergeant, greeting us first thing in the morning in lieu of the traditional alarm clock. They will even be dressed for the part: boots up to the knees, camouflage outfit, that trademark Smokey the Bear hat with the strap tucked tightly under the chin. It is my hope that he or she will "get our heads on straight" before the rigors of the day have a chance to knock us off track.

As we jump out of bed and come to attention, our personal drill sergeant will "get all in our faces," like the infamous Sergeant Carter in the old *Gomer Pyle* show, bellowing out the words that will forever keep us on the straight and narrow: *"Get with it, scum face! You will not live forever! No one is immortal! You can and will die! Make every day count, scum face! You got that? I can't h-e-a-r you! It's a darned good day to die ... oh, and have a real nice day!"*

Chapter 14: They Don't Call It Baggage for Nothin'

IT WAS DURING A weekly session with my therapist at the age of forty that I made the discovery. We were discussing my current job situation, my marital life, and my tour of duty on earth when the conversation came around to what my life was like growing up.

I told her that I was a minister's son and as such I spent a lot of time in the company of other ministers. "Men of the cloth," as you might suspect, tend to be fairly even-tempered individuals with relatively calm dispositions. Life, therefore, was pretty uneventful for me—James Jr.—downright boring at times, you might say. But all things considered, it was a positive kind of boring.

Suffice it to say there were no wild drinking parties or all-night poker games during my youth, I said. If a party was said to be "BYOB" when I was growing up, it most likely meant "Bring Your Own Bible"—not that there's anything wrong with that. The only spirited get-together that I can recall when I was younger was a real rough-and-tumble game of charades that I witnessed at a party one evening when I was about ten. I asked to be included several times in this activity, but I guess it was just a little too intense for me at that age.

Consider, also, that I am an only child and therefore had no brothers or sisters with which to argue or beat on or to pound me senseless. It could be that having to fight for the bathroom on occasion or being able to "rat" on a sibling or struggling for the last piece of chicken during dinner would actually have done me some good. I also realize that my parents seldom argued in front of me when I was young. I'm not saying that they didn't argue; I'm sure they had their share of spats. For whatever reason, they just didn't argue when I was around. The word confrontation, therefore, wasn't in my dictionary. Had I tried to look it up, it would probably have said "See passive."

As the conversation progressed, I was shocked to hear myself compare my early upbringing to one particular episode of the original *Star Trek* television series—I am a semi-Trekkie—that I had seen many times in reruns. If you're a fan of the show, you'll recall that, at the beginning of most episodes, the crew of the Starship Enterprise investigated some urgent distress call on an alien planet. They were then transported down to the foreign world, phasers (weapons) on stun, of course, all in keeping with the "boldly go where no man has gone before" mantra.

Fighting the Effects of Gravity

The common joke among fans of the show was that the shiny, young, wet-behind-the-ears character in the episode—you could pick him or her out immediately because he or she would always be an unfamiliar face, an insignificant ensign making a one-time guest appearance on the show—would then be killed off. The characters had different names, of course, but they could have been given one common title: "Ensign Expendable." As soon as the episode began and I saw this fresh face, I remember saying to myself, *Uh-oh, he's gone.*

What happened next was fairly predictable. After disposing of the fresh-faced ensign, the crew would be taken prisoner by some strange alien-life force. Before long, "Bones" (Dr. McCoy, played by DeForest Kelly) would get emotional and curse Mr. Spock's "green Vulcan blood." Spock (Leonard Nimoy) would tell Bones that his behavior was "illogical." Scotty (the late James Doohan), the engineer, would at some point emphatically announce to the captain in his Scottish brogue the now iconic retort: "Captain, I can't give you no more power!"

The aggressive "Klingons"—the warring race who, while they actually weren't humans, looked a little too African American for my taste—would be lurking about somewhere in the vicinity in their foreboding, maniacal-looking spacecraft for which they had somehow secured the patent for a mysterious "cloaking device"—a bit hard to swallow if you ask me. All this futuristic technology and high-tech wizardry and the mean-spirited African American look-alikes are the only ones with cloaking powers? Flattering in a strange sort of way, but not likely. I digress.

Anyway, this cloaking contraption allowed the Klingon ship to totally disappear from sight at a moment's notice and essentially disrupt an entire episode. The aggressive Klingons were constantly "cloaking" their presence, always lurking about, waiting in the shadows, ready to annihilate anything that moved. And then there was their language—a cross between Ebonics, some Middle-Eastern guttural dialect, and Pig Latin.

Before you could say "Beam me aboard," William Shatner was snuggling up to some green alien woman. Captain Kirk was my space homey, but he could never work as a spokesman for safe sex. He was never terribly concerned about what diseases he could catch from exchanging body fluids with alien "life forms." And there had to be some really nasty ones out there. I tell you, the guy would swap war stories with just about anything.

I told the counselor that, in this particular episode, Captain James T. Kirk and his crew "beamed down" to a planet inhabited by a very docile, sheep-like race of people. They were so meek and unassertive, in fact, that they were like lambs waiting for the slaughter, no match for any aggressive, war-minded invading force. Much to my surprise, I had likened myself to this fictitious, good-natured group of individuals.

Society, I concluded, was more respectful of the Klingon "cloak your spaceship" aggressive mentality than of these passive folks who would allow any low-life space bully to waltz in, seize control of their planet, and steal their lunch money. It was the first time that I had portrayed my upbringing in this manner. My summation was a breakthrough of sorts. I recall my counselor waiting until I finished laughing and shaking my head at the irony of the whole epiphany and then asking me the classic line: "How does that make you feel?" I remember telling her that it made me feel a little silly comparing my life to an episode of *Star Trek* but that it was a cathartic experience nonetheless.

What I discovered that day was that I had gotten a bit of a handle on what makes me tick. I realized that some mental fragments that I had been carrying around with me all of my life had gathered together, followed me into middle age, and become my cross to bear, so to speak. I was simply getting a fix on a piece of my "baggage," a term I had heard thrown around in casual conversation for most of my life. How many times have you heard someone say in passing, "Oh, he's got a lot of baggage?" All of the significant issues that I had yet to address during the first forty years of my life were still hanging around, alive and well in my thoughts.

Having opened my bags, I quickly ascertained that my baggage wasn't all that heavy. My psyche was in pretty good shape, actually,

Fighting the Effects of Gravity

none the worse for the wear. I detected a few dents and dings, but nothing I couldn't smooth out and paint over, nothing that I couldn't get a handle on (excuse the pun). I hadn't grown up being shuffled from one foster home to another or been physically or emotionally abused as a child. But my mental issues seemed worth mentioning nonetheless.

When sizing up my own baggage and why I behave like I do, I also had to consider the fact that my parents have never been considered shrinking violets. My mother, officially known as Dr. Betty H. Robinson, was an accomplished educator, and my father, Rev. Dr. James Robinson Sr., known to many as Jimmie Joe, was a famous athlete in his time who still owns records at the University of Pittsburgh, a minister, and a civil rights activist. They were, and still are, very strong-willed, aggressive individuals. While they were good parents, they cast a mighty large shadow when I was growing up. I never voiced my opinions or intentions until I grew older. I guess I figured, *Hey, these two characters cast one massive shadow; I'll just hide behind it until I reach midlife.* I have also heard similar statements from children of Hollywood celebrities.

I remember shying away from playing high school football because the coach would always assess the possibility of my playing on the team with the words: "If you're half as good as your father ..."

Somehow I could sense, even at this tender age, that this coach's expectations were running a little too hot for my tastes. I never complained or stressed about it, though. I just always managed to be working a summer job during the last two weeks in August, when summer football camps were held. I may have been an innocent and naïve little fellow drowning in the wave of my parent's fame, but I certainly wasn't stupid.

One fall after I missed football camp, I remember a coach lamenting the fact that I didn't come out for football. But I knew what to say. I diplomatically told him that I worked all summer because "I needed the money." That ended the conversation. In truth, I didn't really need the cash, but he seemed impressed that

I was so conscientious that I was willing to work rather than play sports.

I would have to say that society doesn't take kindly to soft-spoken, nonassertive types. A "laid-back" personality may be acceptable, but a quiet one is totally not. When I was younger, I can't count the number of times that someone asked me: "Why are you so quiet?" "Can you speak up?" Or, now that I'm in a drama group, "Can't hear you in the back!"

As a big fan of the show *Seinfeld*, I could point to one particular episode of the show and assume that I could best be classified as a "low talker." I've always thought that, if you could put together society's ideal specimen, it would be a loquacious, beautiful, *intelligent* blonde—Jessica Simpson with an IQ upload.

Once I realized what I needed to do to make myself more assertive in a job interview, I worked hard to bring myself out of my shell. Once, while preparing for an interview, I vowed that I would take it to the interviewer, that I would take control, sell myself, and do whatever was necessary to get noticed. I would jump on the interviewer's desk and sing Al Jolson tunes if that's what it took.

I used various methods to psych myself up all the way to his office. Unfortunately there were no energy drinks available at this time. When I met him, I gave him a firm handshake and sat down on the edge of my seat indicating my eagerness, a trick I picked up from some friends of mine who owned their own company—they hired a candidate because he sat on his chair in this manner. After I landed the job, I had occasion to review the interviewer's notes. His remarks were generally positive, but one of his comments read something to the effect of "Seemed a little quiet, maybe he was nervous."

Upon closer examination of my lightweight luggage, I beheld a virtual 8x10 glossy of all the insecure, overbearing bosses for whom I had ever worked. I thought about all of the times that my integrity, "work ethic," and abilities had been questioned in the working world. The cumulative damage inflicted by my former employers upon my once pristine self-esteem had obviously done some damage. The last five-year stint on my résumé was a job in city politics that tainted me not only on the workplace but on society in general. The long-term corruption and good-old-boy network was quite evident. Let's just say that it's unfortunate that being a decent person and making a living can't always coexist.

No doubt about it, I had laid claim to my own baggage. But more importantly, I had made a surprising discovery, yet another in a long series of profound midlife awakenings. It had taken me to the halfway point in life to learn that it is, quite often, not until individuals reach the middle stages of their being that they finally open their personal suitcases and get to assess the damage for the first time.

Indeed, it seems to me that middle age is often the point when many of us get a real handle on the baggage issue. We finally realize that our physical selves weren't the only casualties of middle age. We sadly admit that our psyches have taken their share of hits as well. Some psyches, as you might expect, take more of a pounding than others.

We also perceive how all the mean-spirited comments made to us over the years—the full-scale verbal abuse as well as the subtle innuendoes—did little damage to our physical being but probably left a few small dents in our sensitive craniums. So much for that old saying about "sticks and stones …"

Oh, All Right Then. But Do We Really Have to Call It Baggage?

When the dust had settled from this latest midlife revelation, one final issue surfaced. While I couldn't dispute the fact that we all tote around our share of emotional pain and that it often affects people in different ways, I take exception to the manner in which we label this load. I had to ask myself, what's the deal with this baggage-speak, anyway? Who first coined this phrase? Whence does this language come? There was something about this term that just didn't sit right.

Sure, the word was suitable for some applications. Sure, one could label my encumbrances as baggage. But who am I to be a barometer for such things? I likened my lingering valises to a 1960s Gene Roddenberry sci-fi television show. I openly discuss a fictitious race of Klingons and masked warships. How much mental trauma could I have accumulated? My problems could probably be shoved into an overnight bag with room for underwear and socks.

But what of the truly serious mental problems that exist out there? What of the disturbing cases of long-term incest or the troublesome instances of parental abuse and neglect? Aren't we minimizing the severity of their problems by lumping them all together and filing them under the heading "baggage?" Aren't we doing these people a disservice? Aren't we suggesting that the immense feeling of violation that a rape victim must feel could somehow be concealed in a stylish, two-piece, trendy collection inspired by one Louis Vuitton or maybe pushed about in one of those wheeled carryons? Do we really want to label this type of trauma as baggage?

It also seems to me that, when we casually whip this term about, we have been selling ourselves short. Perhaps by using this term we have become desensitized. Perhaps this tendency of ours

Fighting the Effects of Gravity

to lump all of our problems together and put them under the heading of "baggage" has hindered our ability to get rid of them. *Oh, it's just baggage,* we thought. Everyone has it. There's nothing anyone can do about it.

So, in the interest of mental health, I call upon all middle-agers to cease and desist when it comes to the infamous "B" word. I say it's time to admit that we have been fooling ourselves. If we are to effectively deal with our burdens, we need to agree that this declaration is woefully inadequate and that every time we use it we're taking the easy way out. We need to readjust our thinking and utilize the proper clinical terminology. We need to come to the conclusion that we're never likely to witness anyone toting a forty-five-inch Pullman into a therapist's office, and that the pain of a divorce can't really be conveniently tossed into a footlocker for storage.

In other words, it's time we grew up and shook this childish moniker once and for all! When speaking to another adult, we don't say "da-da" when we mean "father." We don't say we have to "poo-poo" when we excuse ourselves to go to the bathroom. We all used this type of doublespeak when we were younger, but I think it's safe to say we don't use it these days, at least not when we are speaking to other middle-aged adults. I have heard experts say that adults shouldn't use such euphemisms even when talking to their young children. If you're talking to a child about a dog, then say dog; don't use a cute substitute like "doggie."

When I was a child, my parents, like most parents of that time, insisted that the male organ simply be known as a "doo-dad." But I don't recall using that term in recent years. My children are all girls, so the subject never came up much. But as I recall, we used the proper biological terminology. Had I hit them with my cherished childhood "doo-dad" designation, they would have rolled their eyes and said: "Oh, Daddy!" So we really shouldn't use the expression *baggage* if what we really mean is "mental trauma associated with an abusive upbringing."

In future generations, the word *baggage* should be considered taboo, all but outlawed in this context. Any person, middle-aged or otherwise, heard voicing this word in public from this point on should be strongly cautioned on its use. Your reply to the usage of such casual terminology in social functions should be as follows: "Baggage? You mean those things we use to carry our clothes?"

Having cleared this little language hurdle, I say we begin the task of emptying our bags. Yes, I say it's high time we all came clean. To this end, I wish to take this opportunity to throw down the gauntlet. I want to issue a challenge to all middle-agers to confront their issues, to deal with the weight formerly known as *baggage* in a whole new way.

I submit that the time has come for honesty. I propose that we expand upon the traditional one-on-one, therapist-patient arrangement and initiate a radical new form of group therapy. I even have a catchy name for it: "En Masse Therapy."

As part of "En Masse Therapy," I am urging middle-agers everywhere to wear mental identification tags on their lapels or breast pockets for one specified day of the year. Like the bracelets worn for medical reasons, these ID tags would boldly but silently proclaim your emotional pain; in effect, chase your innermost problems out into the open where they can be rounded up and observed by all.

Just think of the enormous therapeutic value—forty-year-old skeletons being rudely tossed from every closet! Each individual's darkest hours rooted out for all to see—the equivalent of one big, emotional coming-out party. In this manner, each of us could walk a few miles in others' shoes and feel some measure of their pain, turning it into one enormous burden. We could all bear witness to the fact that no one is exempt from what we used to call *baggage* and that everyone has his or her own problems.

Just imagine how much more understanding you might be if you saw a fellow middle-ager displaying the following:

ORPHANED
ABUSED AS A CHILD
DIVORCED
NEVER KNEW MY FATHER
STUCK IN AN ABUSIVE RELATIONSHIP

Fighting the Effects of Gravity

Even ponder, if you will, my own startling revelation:

EARLY CHILDHOOD RESEMBLED A *STAR TREK* EPISODE

After this day of proclamation, these declarations could be removed and ceremoniously discarded forever. It could be a symbolic gesture designed to jump-start the healing process and release us from any harmful liabilities.

Having apprised you of the situation, I leave the ball in your court. If you are truly serious about dumping your emotional load, you should take the first step. I hope you eventually come to the conclusion that your old issues are a liability, a needless burden, in some instances standing between you and the type of person you really want to be. I hope you wake up and realize that politely passing this load off as "baggage" is a cop-out. Don't put it off; there's a lot at stake. You can determine your own destiny. The goal of unencumbered intellectual freedom for the second half of your life is within your grasp.

We don't keep thirty-year-old newspapers around to litter our homes or allow twenty-year-old suits to clutter up our closets. So why drag your negative past around like those invisible friends we all had when we were younger? Recognize it and kick it to the curb! Even if adverse life circumstances have had a positive effect on your life, you still need to acknowledge their impact and recognize them for what they are.

Reclaim your soul. Confront your worst moments and give your unclaimed emotional duffels and knapsacks the old heave-ho. For your own piece of mind, ditch the demons, lose the mental malingers, clean out the closets, stay away from those Klingon types, and whatever you do, don't call it baggage.

Chapter 15: Life Sucks and Then They Give You a Wristwatch

> *I've looked at life from both sides now*
> *from win and lose and still somehow*
> *It's life's illusions I recall*
> *I really don't know life at all.*
> Joni Mitchell

WELL, YOU KNEW THIS all had to come to an end sooner or later. After the falling butts, the doctors, the sweaty, grumpy sex, the disgruntled joints, the failing vision, rumors of death, fear of old age, and an intimate meeting with the Starship Enterprise, I had to end this odyssey somewhere. As it turns out, I would end it all with a particularly profound awakening, the most significant of all wake-up calls. It was during my middle years that I began to receive this strange premonition. It was as if a street evangelist had walked up to me and presented me with my very own personalized brochure of doom:

"Hey, Robinson. You're being had big time. Wake up before it's too late!"

Suddenly, the pieces were all starting to fit. After a lifetime of wearing blinders, I was seeing life's true colors. My mind was clearing; I was definitely onto something big.

I was getting the distinct impression that life as I knew it was not nearly as complicated a proposition as I first thought. I realized that this thing known as life was, in fact, somewhat of a sham, a cheap trick, that there was very little to this exercise that couldn't be summed up in a sentence or two or couldn't be detected by the naked eye.

It was also painfully apparent that all of the subtle implications that pointed to the fact that I was getting shafted had sailed right over my youthful head. Oh, I don't want to be too hard on myself; the clues didn't exactly smack me in the face. No one grabbed me firmly by my shoulders, looked me in the eye, and blurted out that I was being taken for a ride, but there was always some indication that something dastardly was afoot. If only I had paid a little more attention.

In hindsight, I recall those "Life sucks and then you die!" bumper stickers that were displayed so prominently, the "Life's a bitch!" comments that echoed so frequently throughout my life, not to mention all of the casual "Oh well, that's life" remarks I kept hearing. My mother must have made this "Life's a bitch!" pronouncement one hundred times, but it obviously flew into my left ear with all good intentions and scurried out the right ear undetected. In retrospect, maybe she was trying to tell me something.

There was also the sly manner in which I was quietly handed the baton, the way I was cleverly eased into the workforce as a summer employee at a Pittsburgh newspaper at the tender age of fifteen, all the job interviews I endured, the way I was quietly ushered into parenthood at twenty-six.

No hoopla, no big demands, just a gentle push from the frying pan into the fire.

There were those legions of loyal men and women like my late father-in-law, who toiled unselfishly for one company, labored eight or more hours a day for thirty-five to forty years, only to receive a modest company pension and the infamous gold watch at retirement. Before I even truly understood what retirement was all about, I used to think that a gold watch was something

Fighting the Effects of Gravity

special, a fitting final tribute. But having taken a closer look at this common method of honoring employee dedication, this employer send-off, I have come to one conclusion: the watch probably isn't gold plated, and the tribute ... really isn't all that special.

I remember hearing a story about a man who retired after working in a Pittsburgh steel mill for forty years. During his entire career at this mill, as the story goes, he was never late for work and never missed a day due to illness. I'm sure this gentleman was considered the consummate employee and held in high esteem by his employers, but I have to wonder what he ultimately had to show for it.

I recall how my father-in-law worked for one company for thirty-five years, laboring one of three different shifts, a new shift each week. But upon retirement, he received a modest pension of less than $1,000 a month. When he died ten years later, his widow, my mother-in-law, received a fraction of this sum. I remember how he looked forward to retiring and receiving his pension and Social Security but struggled to make it to age sixty-two due to deteriorating health. He died at the age of sixty-nine.

For the most part, he trusted his employer. He had been promised by the coke plant—they produced a number of steel by-products—that employed him that he would have something of substance coming when he retired. I doubt he knew how much his retirement income would be until the time actually came to sever their relationship.

Unfortunately, my father-in-law may have been one of the lucky ones. Consider the misfortune of those poor mortals who didn't survive their working years, who died before they could receive the ceremonial timepiece or were victims of a company-mandated "reduction in work force" before they reached the magic retirement age.

Ponder, if you will, the fate of those loyal folk who worked until the prerequisite age of sixty-two, made extensive post-retirement plans, even sold their homes and purchased expensive motor homes to tour the country in their "golden years," but who unexpectedly died before they could put gas in the tank.

Oh, the cruel irony of it all. Does the term "wake up and smell the coffee" have any relevance here?

No matter; these revelations amounted to nothing more than yesterday's news, water under some old bridge. Happily, after nearly half a century of wearing blinders, I was finally on to the ruse. Granted, I was pushing forty when the light bulb lit, but, hey, better late than never.

Suddenly, my whole take on the inner workings of life had changed. Using my newfound middle-aged insight like a telescope, I could see how it all transpired. I could see exactly how Life, the joker that he is, had been stringing me along, how he had, in effect, lulled me to sleep, how he cons us and we in turn con ourselves into doing his dirty work. I could see how life uses our youthful exuberance and innocence to his advantage.

The deal must have gone down something like this: wearing a weak disguise to mask his true identity—a cheap wig and one of those fake pairs of glasses with the nose, no doubt—the prankster conned me at a young age to do his bidding. Knowing that I was too naïve to ask the right questions, he gave me the impression that there was some intricate game plan lurking beneath the surface that I could refer to whenever I felt the need. "It's there," seemed to be the message. "Just trust me."

I bet you know the story. Perhaps you've had the same feeling at one time or another. Life, like the ever-tricky blowfish, seems to blow himself up to look considerably more impressive than he really is, all the while cleverly concealing the fact that we are getting nowhere fast. We then keep the scam going like the trusting souls that we are. By the time we catch on to the shenanigans, we're blowing out forty to fifty candles—too late, life figures, to do anything about it. Sure, he grants us some latitude to make a few decisions along the way, but he knows we'll fall in line. He knows we'll play his little game.

It was my moment of truth. No longer just casual acquaintances, Mr. Life and I had been formally introduced. Actually, it wasn't quite what you would call a formal introduction—more like one of those fraternity hazings. Here's how it went: extending his hand as if to make my acquaintance, that Life character zapped me with one of those lame, shock-buzzer gags and then quickly motioned for me to come closer just so he could squirt me in my naïve face with that fake lapel flower.

As I wiped the remnants of the prank from my shocked visage, he treated me to a few choruses of "I Never Promised You a Rose Garden" (asking for my participation on the chorus) and then put his arm on my shoulder and softly whispered the coup de grâce into my ear. "Welcome to reality," he spoke with a sly grin. "And don't go looking for any of those silver linings. I'm afraid that this is as good as it gets."

Okay, so perhaps I overdramatize a bit, but more than anything else we should all be struck by the unfairness of it all. We should be asking ourselves, where is the justice? After all, most of us baby boomers have done our part. We came along after World War II and carried the torch. We were law-abiding citizens, prize pupils. We did everything asked of us: we played by the rules, we ate our vegetables, we respected our elders. We went to church every Sunday and worshiped the God of our choice if we believed. We kept the résumé to one page. We stayed out of jail (for the most part). We all worked the perfunctory forty hours a week. We paid our dues, and where did it get us?

Like my father-in-law and the other trusting folks who worked three-quarters of their lives for a Swiss timepiece and a handshake, we had been subtly led to believe that there was a reward in the offing, that something meaningful was waiting for us at the end of this road. We then deluded ourselves into believing that this fantasy was gospel. We convinced ourselves that we had to play the game to survive. We now had to suffer the consequences. We had to face the prospect that we wouldn't be getting a whole heckuva lot in return for a lifetime of diligence.

Oh sure, we had a little more money. We were probably worth considerably more than we were twenty years ago, but that was of little comfort. What good is plain old currency when your life is on the line? What can money do for you when the remainder of your existence is hanging in the balance?

Consider me an innocent victim of circumstances. Life wasn't really that complicated; it just seemed that way in my youth. My bedroom, when I was living in my family's first house in 1965, seemed enormous at the time. But when I returned to this house one day when I was older and banged my head on the low-hanging ceiling light, I quickly realized just how small my seemingly huge room really was. Once you get past the smoke and mirrors, you see life for what it truly is in all of its simplicity.

In the final analysis, I was simply too absorbed in the process of living my life—raising my children, paying bills, and keeping my marriage afloat—to even consider the possibility that I was getting the short end of the stick. I was too naïve to push my own agenda; too busy putting food on the table to realize that life was eating my lunch. Like the first five months of salary that we earn every calendar year is said to pay our debt to Uncle Sam, so the first forty or fifty years of our lives can sometimes be chalked up to experience. The score at the end of the first half of play seemed a bit lopsided, something along the lines of Life: 40; the Robinson guy: zip.

If you feel as if you've played life to a dead heat in the first half and your score is closer to 40-40, I feel good for you. You've beaten the trickster at his own game. But for me it was a defining moment.

Fighting the Effects of Gravity

My days of playing the game by life's rules were over. I suddenly realized that just maybe I wasn't cut out for a traditional "job." The die had been cast. I had gone out in search of a traditional solution and run smack-dab into my own individuality. Something had to give. Sooner or later I would have to discard the traditional mold that had been my beacon for most of my life and fashion one of my own. I was quickly becoming my own man.

So Much for That Meaning of Life Notion

Don't look now, but this little midlife discovery puts a real crimp into the so-called "meaning of life" debate, that commonly held belief that somewhere in this universe there exists a supreme logic, an ultimate answer. I think that most of us, at one time or another, have conjured up this image of a mystical figure with long, flowing, gray-and-black locks and an angelic demeanor, sitting cross-legged and meditating on some faraway mountaintop, holding the magical trump card that will set us all free. When we picture this fellow, we hear sitar music and smell incense burning. Who knows where this image comes from, who plants it in our heads.

Well, don't look now, but I think the guru has finally spoken. My guess is that he got the word out in written form via fax or e-mail or some slick press release. In case you missed it, I figure it looked something like this:

FOR IMMEDIATE RELEASE

"Life sucks; then you die!
Have an incredibly mystical day!"
Hugs and kisses,
The Guru

Fighting the Effects of Gravity

No doubt about it—the jig is up. It's time we got used to the idea that there is no mystery to life, no all-encompassing meaning hiding at the epicenter of this existence. As comedian Flip Wilson used to say, "What you see is what you get." And even then, there is nothing to indicate that what we are seeing is exactly what we will continue to get.

I doubt we'll ever find that elaborate reason that will explain why we're here, no profound explanation for why we've been running around like headless chickens for the better part of our lives, and no justification whatsoever for why that annoying static cling keeps making our pants get all hung up on our socks. Further, we will probably never fully understand why Dick Clark was able to look so young for so long.

It's high time we face the music. It now appears that our existence is highly individualized, based largely on the do-it-yourself concept. In other words, if you as a midlifer are patiently waiting for some manner of quick fix, some clue that will magically superglue this whole thing together, don't hold your breath. It would be nice if there were more to this existence, but I'm afraid there's not. I am now firmly convinced that the word *life* is nothing more than a secret code, a clever way of saying, "Don't call me; I'll call you." In the immortal words of the brilliant Porky Pig: "Th-th-th-that's all, folks!"

Besides, who were we kidding? Weren't we really deluding ourselves with that "meaning of life" theory, anyway? Let's just imagine for a moment that this was, in fact, all leading to something. Do you honestly think that it would have remained a secret this long? Wouldn't we be fairly well inundated with that little bit of wisdom by now?

It appears likely that, in a "tell it all" society such as ours, we would have seen this alleged meaning everywhere we looked: scrawled on countless walls, immortalized on thousands of bumper stickers, displayed on T-shirts, and used in the form of a question on *Jeopardy!* Psychics would have commercialized the truth by now, fashioning it to look like a customized AAA "triptik" with our own personal route to utopia highlighted in yellow. A crafty paparazzi, utilizing one of those huge, state-of-the-art telephoto lenses, would surely have snapped a revealing photo of our infamous guru on his mountain retreat by this time and sold it for a small fortune.

We know which celebrities are about to tie the knot, thanks to those snoopy helicopters with the powerful cameras circling above the "secret" wedding sites. We have journalists who will get information any way they can, including sifting through celebrity garbage cans. We hire private detectives to snoop on our spouses. We put hidden cameras behind mirrors in dressing rooms of retail stores to ensnare shoplifters and in our own homes to catch nannies in the act of abusing our children.

When war erupted in the Caribbean nation of Grenada in 1983, the news media were on the "secret" beach invasion site with cameras and lights, filming the American soldiers as they (the soldiers) landed. Can you imagine journalists and news crews occupying the beaches at Normandy before the troops in WWII? I guess the intense enemy fire would have cooled their enthusiasm a bit.

It's hard to imagine that, back in the sixties, President John F. Kennedy was serenaded with that now-famous, breathy "Happy Birthday" number by Marilyn Monroe, whom it now seems pretty obvious he knew intimately, and the press actually turned their heads to this indiscretion. Imagine how this prominent tryst would be handled in the present-day, can't-keep-a-secret goldfish bowl.

No, we've obviously allowed ourselves to get caught up in the hype. It's quite apparent to me now that life is your basic one-step exercise, something simple in the order of "every man for himself."

Life, it now seems to me, is a fairly straightforward concept, darned-near boring if you think about it. Simply put, life is about living and responsibilities, people like you and me thrown together and forced to coexist as best we can. Life is about birth and marriage, children and debt, and old age and death. Life is about savoring the good times while they last and doing our best

Fighting the Effects of Gravity

to weather the storms that may arise. Life is about setting a course and dealing with whatever may come your way. As the late Beatle John Lennon once said in the form of a lyric, "Life is what happens to you while you're busy making other plans."

When you reach the middle part of this life, you tend to realize that it is we, the prisoners, who have the ultimate control. It's the inhabitants who have the power to make the rules. We set this thing up, for the most part. Life is like a big Mr. Potato Head. We can fashion it to look any way we want.

While there are elements in life that we can't control—whom we're born to and whether or not we die, to name a couple—there are certainly many events that are within our command. We just don't take advantage. We let our circumstances call the shots. We let "life" dictate how we should live. No, it's time to face facts. We've been swindled, bamboozled, hustled. We've fallen for the old bait-and-switch. The truth is, if you want to get any more from your existence, you'll have to extract it yourself. As Tom Lehrer once said, "Life is like a sewer. What you get out of it depends on what you put in it." If there is a deeper meaning to this life, it hits you around the time that you discover that there is no deeper meaning to this life.

The Liberation. And a Big Shout-Out to Jimmy Durante

Having come face-to-face with the reality of it all, I could envision my life going off into any number of directions. I could see myself demonstrating any one of the following stunned reactions:

- **Stunned Reaction #1:** I could settle. I could become a casual observer for the remainder of this performance. I could throw up my hands in disgust, telling all who would listen what I would do if I had it all to do over again (a fairly silly supposition if you ask me).
- **Stunned Reaction #2:** I could slip on a pair of blinders. Yes, take the easy way out. I've known people who would ignore the findings and go on as if nothing has happened. They would continue to play the game, despite the overwhelming evidence that someone has made off with the ball, announcing to all, in effect, "I didn't see anyone get had, did you see anyone get had?"
- **Stunned Reaction #3:** I could simply lose it and go off the deep end. God forbid I follow in the footsteps of the infamous disgruntled postman and go on a rampage, thinking that this action would somehow soothe my battered ego.

But the truth is that I would be taking the bait. I would be playing right into Life's hands. Utilizing any one of these strategies would be a monumental step in the wrong direction (not to mention an incredible waste of time and ammo). Oh, sure, I could spend the rest of my life in denial, but who would I be hurting except myself? While there's nothing stopping me from laying waste to an entire office full of ex-cronies, what would it get me? (Besides an extended stay on death row.)

Fighting the Effects of Gravity

No, call me crazy, but I see a better way. I've actually spotted a seldom-used loophole in this contract. Perhaps I'm one of those idealists who perceive the philosophical bottle as being half full rather than half empty, but I think when you reach middle age, a most definitive window of opportunity presents itself. I see something positive in all of this. The fact that we've been left for dead can actually work to our advantage.

Once you get over the shock, you begin to see this juncture of life for what it truly is: a beginning, not an end, a door opening rather than a door closing. It's all in how you look at it. Something tells me that, despite all of the evidence to the contrary, we haven't been had after all—we've actually been liberated!

If you haven't organized a mutiny already, I think of middle age as the optimal time to hijack this vessel and begin assuming control of your own life. It appears that we have it all wrong. Middle age is not the time to throw in the towel; it's the time to scrap the old towel and find one more to your liking.

Midlife is the time to snatch the reins, the time to adapt the rules to fit your agenda, the time to put into action all of the plans that have been collecting dust on your personal back burner all these years. Middle age is the ultimate moment of truth, the time to put up or shut up. Midlife is the time to wrestle control away from your captors and empower yourself.

What better signpost than midlife to use to dust off those old dreams? To start that business, to go back and finish college or earn that second degree, to get serious about that writing career. You've heard all those annoying parables that sit prominently on desks and hang on walls but never really make sense (much less provide inspiration), truisms like: "Life is what you make it." "He who laughs last, laughs best." And that confusing one that suggests that "the tough get going when the going gets tough."

Well, now you know what they're talking about. Get going, get tough, get a grip, for God's sake. Stop thinking that you lost the game. Look at all of the people who have been living all of these years and have been winning the game, playing by their own rules. How could you even consider yourself a serious participant all these years when you've only now managed to figure out the rules?

I see middle-aged people every day who have gotten the message. I can tell from their demeanor that the light bulb has lit, that they finally understand how the game is played. They seem to have a new attitude. They're more confident and more relaxed. Having figured out by midlife that they can play the game any way they want, many individuals work out a severance deal with a long-time employer and retire while still in their fifties or accept an early-retirement offer that affords them more time with their families. Some employees quit their high-paying but high-stress jobs and step out on their own, taking a leap of faith in an effort to have more control over their lives.

A friend of mine has become a consultant and performs the same services that she did for a large company but is willing to assume the risk to be able to do it her own way. Some employees grow disillusioned with the corporate lifestyle and take a job in midlife that is less lucrative but more satisfying and with fewer hours, while others perform volunteer work. I know of a doctor who quit medicine in midlife and began performing in piano bars. My children's first pediatrician began taking acting classes in his seventies because that's what he always wanted to do. He felt compelled to be a doctor because that was what his parents wanted.

I see others who seem as if they have known the score all along. Although I have spoken mainly about those who have struggled throughout their lives and have never reached a sense of fulfillment, perhaps you are on the flip side of the coin. Perhaps you have reached midlife and consider yourself to have lived a life of meaning and success. Maybe you have achieved a level of fulfillment that many haven't. But maybe you also find yourself staring into the face of middle age with the same doubts and fears as those who have struggled along the way. As Bruce Willis said to a police officer under fire from ruthless terrorists in his first *Die Hard* movie, "Welcome to the party, pal!"

Fighting the Effects of Gravity

No matter what perspective we come with, we all have something in common. You may not realize this, but life doesn't begin in earnest until you've been smacked around a bit. It's not until you've been whacked a few times by the blatant unfairness of it all that you begin to get the true picture. It's only when you're sitting on the floor wondering who just yanked the rug out from under you that the real fun begins.

Consider my situation for a moment. Middle age was indeed the turning point in my life. Falling buttocks and arches aside, for me, midlife was, in many ways, when my life began. But when the notion of authoring a book about middle age came to me, I soon realized that things were different this time around. As I began to write, a new style emerged. Apparently, as I reached my early forties, profound changes in my writing style would serve to bolster the profound changes that I was going through in midlife—my awareness of my own mortality and my place in the grand scheme of things.

These intense beginnings would not only guide me through this project but through the rest of my life. Forty-two years of living would be my wellspring of expertise, my base of support. Surviving to my early forties, as it turns out, was all I needed to break ground on a new beginning, to initiate my life's work. Surviving to the age of fifty-eight would turn out to be enough time to lay the finishing touches on my first project.

If you aren't drawn to Christianity, my belief has always been that everyone needs to hold on to something bigger than themselves—something to pray to or ascribe to or to just lean on—be it a higher power; a higher set of beliefs; *"Que sera, sera. Whatever will be, will be"*; yoga; kismet; astrology; something that takes the pressure off; something that frees you from believing that you are in this alone, that you have to do everything yourself. Whatever support system you might believe in, hold on to it and don't let go.

Perhaps your life at middle age is not as meaningful as you would like it to be. Well, it's not too late to do something about it. Don't tell me you'll have more time when the kids have gone off to college. Don't put it off; you're not promised that much time. I challenge you to find the time to do what your heart tells you and to do it as soon as possible. I challenge you to find out what your passion is and make it the centerpiece of your earthly existence. I challenge you to make your dream a reality now!

But if you want to make the most of your time, you'll have to alter the way in which you do business. It seems likely that, if you're going to get anywhere in the second half of this endeavor, you're going to have to put yourself first once in a while. That's right—you're going to have to get a little selfish. This might sound like a totally foreign concept, but I'm asking you, in effect, to make a U-turn in the middle of the highway. From now on, you're going to have to think of yourself first, to do things your way: pursue your passions, get in touch with your higher power, find out what makes you tick, learn what floats your boat, and go after it with a vengeance. You'll have to, as we used to say in the wild sixties, do your own thing.

No, now don't get all self-centered on me. I'm just asking you to elevate your earthly agenda to a higher level. Like me, perhaps you have ignored your needs in deference to the needs of your family and your work. From this point forward, the recipe for happiness is as follows: take care of yourself first and the rest will fall in place.

By this I don't mean to be totally selfish and ignore the needs of everyone else. I mean that if you take care of your spiritual needs, your dreams, and your personal desires first, you will feel better about yourself and then in turn will be more suited to deal with the needs of others.

Don't worry about the scoreboard. That 40–0 whitewash is meaningless at this stage of the game. It simply doesn't apply to you. Consider your first forty years to be like an exhibition season. Amnesty is the new order of the day, like the window that is opened on occasion to provide delinquent book-borrowers the opportunity to return overdue books with no questions asked, all debts forgiven. We're back to 0–0.

Fighting the Effects of Gravity

By all accounts, you're just getting warmed up. Consider midlife your second wind, a stay of execution. Life has just handed you your walking papers. You're free! You just don't know it yet. So put that helmet on and get back in the game. Quit feeling sorry for yourself. The best is still to come. According to the latest actuarial tables, we may have as many as forty years left in the hopper, plenty of time to get our acts together.

If you follow my advice, you'll see an immediate difference. Before you know it, you'll be your own person, dining alone at the top of life's food chain. You'll be calling your own shots, whistling your own tune, living life on your terms. No need for name-calling or violent retribution. By going your own way, you will have already made the ultimate statement, the most emphatic of rebellious gestures. You will have, in symbolic fashion, of course, turned your back to life, dropped your trousers, and grabbed your knees in a magnificent display of quiet defiance.

If you've already lived your life on your own terms, then I raise my glass to you. You have a head start; you're ahead of the game. Like the teams with the best records come playoff time, you have a bye week. But you still have some work to do. You, like all of us, still have unanswered questions about your mortality to address, and you still have to work to make the second half of your life the best that it can be.

To all of us who have lived the first half of this contest and who are currently fighting the effects of gravity, I say, "Bravo! Keep up the good work!" You have fought the good fight, withstood the forces of gravity, and done so with dignity and honor. You are dealing with the doctors and the exams that we so badly need at this time of our lives. You're handling your new sexual roles, putting up with those muscle aches and pains, coping with the sting of arthritis, and stemming the tide of presbyopia—bifocals, in case you've forgotten. You're winning the battle with the dreaded brain cramp. You're staring into the face of old age and death and not backing down, and you're kicking that baggage to the curb. You're fighting all the right fights and winning the wars. I'll see you at the next level, my friends. Old age awaits. I feel confident that you'll handle it with a smile and a newfound strength. And it will look good on you.

So let's not waste any more time. With the road to better days plowed and cleared and your head on straight, the time has come for us to get down to serious business. Set the wheels in motion today that will make part two of your life an unqualified success from your point of view.

Farewell, my friends; this is where we part company. And in the immortal words of the late Jimmy Durante, I say, "Good night Mrs. Calabash, wherever you are."

Made in the USA
Lexington, KY
21 February 2012